"Dr. Kurtz offers an illustrative, comprehensive and meaningful approach to reflective practice. Learning opportunities abound from reading the rich examples to applying the model to a healthcare setting."

—Nicholas Ladany, Dean of the School of Leadership, University of San Diego, USA

"Dr. Kurtz brings her wealth of clinical expertise and experience to this excellent new book. While it is an eminently practical manual, grounded within NHS culture and steeped in clinical practice, it is also clearly underpinned by the relevant theoretical influences and empirical research. This makes it an important new addition to the field of Reflective Practice, which is long overdue. I wish it had been available to me!"

— Delia Cushway, Emeritus Professor of Clinical Psychology, Coventry University, UK

"If you want to explore group reflective practice this book is essential reading for nurses and other healthcare professionals. In today's pressured healthcare environment, reflective practice has never been more important to provide time to think and learn. This book and the Intersubjective Model of Reflective Practice opens up new possibilities."

—Dave Clarke, Foundation Professor of Nursing, University of Leicester, UK

"Arabella Kurtz makes a compelling case for the place of reflective practice in healthcare settings and in the training of healthcare professionals. She has drawn on her considerable experience as well as theory to produce a clear Intersubjective Model for reflective practice. Each stage of the model is described in separate chapters which provide excellent guidance and examples of what to do as a facilitator. The first stage deals uniquely with the organisational and contractual issues that so often interfere with the establishment and effective running of reflective groups. The remaining stages guide the reader through the essential tasks of reflective groups. If services are to develop a culture of compassionate care then reflective practice should be integral and this book provides a model for how this could be achieved."

—Tony Lavender, Emeritus Professor of Clinical Psychology, Canterbury Christ Church University, UK

"Reflective practice is increasingly proffered as a panacea to the pressures on healthcare staff of rising clinical demand, financial austerity and a target driven culture, yet it is poorly defined and often difficult to implement. Based on years of working with the lived experience of practitioners in an extensive range of settings, Kurtz has developed a unique, yet widely applicable, intersubjective model of reflective practice integrating experiential, psychoanalytic and phenomenological approaches. By allowing a space for intuition, emotional responsiveness and creativity to develop, staff groups are facilitated in deepening their understanding of human relationships and finding meaning in their work. This book offers an accessible, practical and much-needed guide to reflective practice which will be relevant to all disciplines working in health and social care services."

—Jessica Yakeley, Consultant Psychiatrist in Forensic Psychotherapy and Director of the Portman Clinic, Tavistock and Portman NHS Foundation Trust, UK

How to Run Reflective Practice Groups

In *How to Run Reflective Practice Groups: A Guide for Healthcare Professionals*, Arabella Kurtz explores the use of reflective practice in the modern healthcare context.

Responding to the rapidly increasing demand for reflective practice groups in healthcare and drawing on her extensive experience as a facilitator and trainer, Kurtz presents a fully developed, eight-stage model: the Intersubjective Model of Reflective Practice Groups. The book offers a guide to the organisation, structure and delivery of group sessions, with useful suggestions for overcoming commonly-encountered problems and promoting empathic relationships with clients and colleagues.

Clearly and accessibly written, using full situational examples for each stage of the presented model, *How to Run Reflective Practice Groups* offers a comprehensive guide to facilitating reflective practice in healthcare.

Arabella Kurtz is a consultant clinical psychologist and psychoanalytic psychotherapist. She held jobs in National Health Service (NHS) adult and forensic mental health services, and now works on the University of Leicester Clinical Psychology Training Programme and in private practice.

How to Run Reflective Practice Groups
A Guide for Healthcare Professionals

Arabella Kurtz

Routledge
Taylor & Francis Group

LONDON AND NEW YORK

First published 2020
by Routledge
2 Park Square, Milton Park, Abingdon, Oxon OX14 4RN

and by Routledge
52 Vanderbilt Avenue, New York, NY 10017

Routledge is an imprint of the Taylor & Francis Group, an informa business

© 2020 Arabella Kurtz

British Library Cataloguing in Publication Data
A catalogue record for this book is available from the British Library

Library of Congress Cataloging-in-Publication Data
A catalog record has been requested for this book

ISBN: 978-0-8153-6213-5 (hbk)
ISBN: 978-0-8153-6214-2 (pbk)
ISBN: 978-1-351-11299-4 (ebk)

Typeset in Times New Roman
by Taylor & Francis Books

Contents

Tables

Dedication

To my parents, Antony and Zarrina Kurtz, both doctors in
the UK National Health Service

Acknowledgements

My mother, Zarrina Kurtz, gave me Donald Schon's *The Reflective Practitioner* many years ago, and I am pleased to be able to dedicate this book on reflective practice in healthcare to my father and to her.

A big thank you is due to Glenys Parry, who has acted as my writing buddy, discussing early ideas for the book and providing editorial input throughout. Glenys advised me at the start to write a practical book, which for the reader would be as much as possible like attending a live training event. This was good advice, and the book is a lot less dry than it would have been if I had not had this steer from her.

I owe a debt of gratitude to colleagues on the Leicester clinical psychology training course, who encouraged me years ago to develop a reflective practice seminar programme and have facilitated groups alongside me ever since. They are: Jerry Burgess, Jon Crossley, Kate Duckworth, Jo Herdman, Steve Melluish, Gareth Morgan, Mary O'Reilly, Helen Reader and Alison Tweed. I would also like to thank four colleagues from outside the course, with whom I have co-facilitated groups. They are: Bob Diamond, David Connelly, Jules Jackson and Jo Scordellis. The groups have all been very different from each other, and I have learnt a great deal from my co-facilitators and the trainees each time we embarked on a reflective journey.

I would like to acknowledge the goodwill and creativity of the trainees in the group I co-facilitated with Jo Scordellis from 2016 to 2019, and the group facilitated by Suki Bassey and Emma Tilbury from 2014 to 2017. They generously agreed for their reflective discussions to be the subject of Anya Biggins' and Mark Loveder's doctoral research studies, and to be interviewed and have meetings audiotaped. I learnt a lot from supervising Anya and Mark's in-depth analysis of members' experiences of the groups, and from the alternative perspective brought to thinking about reflective practice through the research lens. I am also grateful to Jo, Suki and Emma for supporting Anya and Mark's research endeavours so wholeheartedly.

I am thankful to those colleagues who helped me set up the Reflective Practice Research Network in the East Midlands. They are: Nicola Anderton, Peter Beardsworth, Suzanne Elliot, Claire Hemming, Kate Partridge and Amandeep Samrai. I have greatly appreciated the relaxed but stimulating atmosphere of this group of busy clinical colleagues, and the contributions they have made to my thinking about many different aspects of reflective practice in the UK National Health Service.

Thanks are due to reflective colleagues Heather Wood and Delia Cushway, who gave valuable feedback on the book at the peer review stage, and to Jo Levene, who provided useful comments on the Generation chapter. Jill Vites taught me a great deal, and lent me a copy of Gosling and Turquet's classic book on small training groups, which I have gone back to again and again. Kathy Fordham has been a skilled co-facilitator of training days on how to run reflective practice groups, and a valuable source of information on models of reflective learning other than Schon's. Penny Lorriman offered technical expertise to help me produce the diagram of the model.

Thanks are also due to painter and friend Kate Giles, who generously allowed me to use her beautiful painting of an illumination on the book cover.

Finally, my heartfelt thanks go to my family, my husband Nick Everett and my children Eben, Michael and Kezia, for their ongoing support and encouragement. They have put up with inevitable periods of preoccupation with writing, and have been both humorous and insightful about the intrusion of reflective practice into their lives.

Note on terms and use of examples from practice

The terms client and patient are both in common usage within healthcare services and have been used at different points depending on the context.

I have taken care to ensure the anonymity of the clients and staff members referred to in the examples given in the book. In my descriptions I have tried to keep the essence of experiences of facilitation of reflective practice, but I have fictionalised elements of the material and put together composite accounts to protect the identities of those referred to. In most cases, I have sought consent from colleagues to include examples of their work, and conferred with them to generate anonymous accounts. Where this was not possible, I have taken additional care to make sure people remain unidentifiable.

1 Introduction

The world we live in is increasingly fast-paced, and it can often feel as if there is not enough time to think. We can all experience pressure to keep up with the speed of change and innovation, and can find ourselves becoming busier and busier without having much of a sense of why we are doing what we are doing. Digital technologies have brought many benefits; they have greatly increased the range and speed of our communications and have also raised expectations as to how quickly work can be done and answers can be found to our questions. Reflective practice provides a necessary corrective in the working environment to this fast, active and reactive aspect of our lives. It aims to help us with questions to which there is no easy or straightforward answer, and also to generate new questions in order to better frame our thinking about novel and complex situations.

This book is about the application of reflective practice in healthcare. Science and technology have a vital role to play in the delivery of healthcare services. However, clinical practice offers up many unique and ambiguous situations which require intuition, judgement and creativity if they are to be handled properly. When these situations are approached in an automatic way, relying too much on standard or pre-existing methods and procedures, they may at best be only superficially resolved and at worst important aspects may be missed and interventions go wrong. There is an art and a science to doing good clinical work.

Reflective practice was first coined as a phrase by the American town planner Donald Schon in his 1980s book *The Reflective Practitioner* and is in frequent usage nowadays in the education and healthcare fields (Schon, 1983). But it is not a recent idea, at least not in its essence. In many ways, reflective practice draws on ancient wisdom and common sense. The influence of the Socratic method, for example, lives on in its emphasis on exploring questions and areas of uncertainty, and on following up on hunches and moments of intuition. Reflective practice owes a debt to the focus in classical philosophy on asking better and more penetrating questions in order to establish a firm basis for critical inquiry. There is also Aesop's (1998) traditional moral tale of 'The tortoise and the hare', which is for me a fable about the value of slowing down to think in a fast-paced world. In this tale, it is the slow, deliberate tortoise who gets to the finishing line ahead of the quick but foolhardy hare. The result of the race is an unexpected one, just as reflective practice often yields surprising results, in the sense that these results are not pre-set and therefore can rarely be anticipated. And to continue with animal metaphors: the often-invoked image of a headless chicken running around in circles vividly conveys how caught up we can get in a relentless round of activity if we do not take time to think, and how this can result in the loss of any real direction and purpose.

In modern healthcare organisations, reflective practice generally occurs in a group setting, and involves taking the time for staff to think about the serious, complex and emotionally charged work they do in caring for those in pain and distress. It requires resources to do it properly, and can seem like an unaffordable luxury when demand on clinical services is high and resources are stretched to the limit. But the cost of not doing so, certainly in the long-term, is immeasurably higher. It stands to reason that high levels of clinical activity without sufficient space to consider actions, process responses and draw on the support and encouragement of colleagues, will result in a sense of isolation amongst staff, burnout and poor or at least much less than optimal clinical practice. Indeed, research has shown us that healthcare staff are particularly at risk of burnout and compassion fatigue, and that these are associated with an increased risk of clinical errors, reduced capacity in staff for empathy and engagement with clients and higher rates of staff absence and turnover (Hall et al., 2016; Edwards et al., 2006). It has also been established that high-quality clinical supervision (and I would include reflective practice under this heading) is associated with increased staff well-being and job satisfaction, and reduced burnout (Hyrkas, 2005; Berg, Hansson & Hallberg, 1994). Furthermore, there is now a growing body of work which shows that high-quality clinical supervision is directly associated with positive clinical outcomes, particularly when the culture of the organisation is supportive of supervisory activity (Bambling et al., 2006; Bradshaw, Butterworth & Mairs, 2007; White & Winstanley, 2010).

What is reflective practice and what is reflective practice in a group?

Simply put, reflective practice is a form of in-depth thinking about work activity with the aim of developing as a practitioner. The concept of reflective practice has its origins in early twentieth-century phenomenological philosophy and the work of a diverse group of philosophers and psychologists including John Dewey, Kurt Lewin, Maurice Merleau-Ponty and William James. These figures had in common an interest in the nature of human thought and reasoning, and the view that a full engagement with experience – the messy, complex and surprising business of living as opposed to abstract ideas about living – is intrinsic to the learning process. John Dewey's seminal work *How We Think* is concerned with understanding and defining critical thought (Dewey, 1910). This type of thought involves reflection on experience, a process whereby ideas about the world and how it works are tested and modified by as full and open engagement with lived experience as possible. His ideas are influential in pedagogy to this day and lie behind widely used reflective teaching models, such as Kolb's experiential learning cycle and Gibbs' stages of reflection (Kolb, 2015; Gibbs, 1988).

In *The Reflective Practitioner*, Schon made a case for the reintegration of intuition and reflexivity into professional practice, which he thought had been squeezed out by a narrow focus on technological expertise. He argued for the introduction of a form of creative and outside-the-box thinking about individual cases, which he called reflective practice, to counter the dominance of standardised, technological approaches (Schon, 1983). Schon described how reflection-on-action, meaning a kind of problem-solving based on close retrospective attention to the details of specific work experiences and the use of diverse thinking and creative methods to understand them, leads to reflection-in-action, and a new form of rigor in professional practice to complement scientific and technological approaches.

Since the 1990s in the United Kingdom, there has been a growing interest in the use of reflective practice in healthcare, especially amongst nurses and clinical psychologists. It has been recognised that the application of even the most up-to-date scientific evidence will only take us so far in the care and understanding of unique and complex human beings, and we need to have space to think creatively in order to apply our knowledge in a way which is relevant to the individual in context (Esterhuizen & Howatson-Jones, 2019; Stedmon & Dallos, 2009; Lavender, 2003). What happens in reflective practice groups in healthcare has been much influenced by other forms of group activity carried out in the health and social care settings, such as staff support, psychoanalytic work discussion groups, and group and systemic therapy. Healthcare staff in the UK are very used to working in groups and teams. The positive side to this is that staff are able to draw on a rich diversity of experiences and knowledge of a variety of theories and techniques. The negative side is that boundaries between reflective practice groups and other types of group can sometimes become unhelpfully blurred.

Construction of a model of group reflective practice has inevitably involved pinning my colours to the mast in terms of my understanding of what reflective practice is and what it is not. My definition is one that I have to some extent discovered, by which I mean that it emerged through a description of what I do, rather than as an abstract or ready-made concept. In my view, reflective practice in groups should have a clear focus on clinical practice and on developing thinking in the work situation. It should be wide-ranging in its means and methods, making use of the resources of the group – intellectual, imaginative and emotional – to open up perspectives and access new ways of thinking about clinical challenges and dilemmas. It is rooted in the lived experience of practitioners, who then work together, from the ground up, to build an understanding of what is going on. It has an emphasis on the human and relational aspects of the caring work we do, and on bringing intuitive and emotional understanding back into the healthcare frame. It also, in contrast to individual supervision of a reflective kind, aims to develop the capacity of the group to use peer support and create a more reflective working culture: an environment in which colleagues are better able to draw on each other for support and development of their thinking about clinical cases on a day-to-day basis.

The methods used by the group to open up thinking about practice may be diverse, but the overall focus should clearly be on helping members with the working task. That is, in my view reflective practice is decidedly not personal therapy. The main reasons colleagues have given over the years for negative experiences of reflective practice are a lack of clarity regarding its purpose, and feeling unsafe because of a perceived expectation of pressure for members to divulge personal information without a rationale for doing this – or, I should add, an ethical basis. One of the main activities of the facilitator of a reflective practice group is to communicate a strong sense of the purpose of the group, and the boundaries around the reflective task. As a qualification to this, I should add that moment-by-moment, or session-by-session, these boundaries are not always clear, particularly if the group is becoming more adventurous and explorative in its thinking. However, the facilitator will create a great deal of safety for group members if they remain grounded in their sense of the aim of reflective practice in the work context, allowing experimentation in thought and feeling but always bringing the group back to what this might mean for the development of practice.

Some words about the modern healthcare context

Those working in senior posts in clinical services receive increasing numbers of requests for staff to offer reflective practice groups to colleagues. These requests arrive in all shapes and sizes: they come from managers on behalf of staff on the ground, especially when levels of sickness and absence are high, and from staff who are overwhelmed by clinical demands and themselves recognise that they are in need of a thinking space; they come from staff in both mental and physical health services, and in the latter case, perhaps, particularly from those working in palliative care and with sick children; they come from staff who work closely together, sharing patients and common clinical dilemmas, and from those who are more isolated and want to access the help and support of a group of colleagues; and they come from those practicing in the community or in out-patient services, and from multidisciplinary or nursing teams in in-patient settings and secure services.

Why has the demand for reflective practice grown so much? On the positive side, the increase is largely the result of the development of emotional literacy and awareness of mental health issues in society as a whole. Admired and well-known figures are bravely opening up and talking to the media about their psychological difficulties and areas of vulnerability. And business academics and entrepreneurs are advocating a new style of collaborative leadership which aims to foster psychological safety and open communication (Edmondson & Verdin, 2018). Healthcare organisations generally still operate in a bureaucratic and a top-down way, but it is much more possible than before to talk with colleagues about the emotional impact of work and to share problems and vulnerabilities.

Despite these social developments, staff in many modern healthcare organisations are often overworked and highly stressed. Awareness of the need to focus on human relationships in our work environments may in one sense never have been greater. But when it comes to modern healthcare organisations, it has also perhaps partly come about as a reaction to the gross undervaluing of relational thinking that has characterised the introduction and consolidation of a somewhat old-fashioned, hard business model. The increase in requests for reflective practice comes, at least in part, as a corrective to the marketisation of healthcare, and in particular, the intense focus on cutting costs and meeting short-term budgetary targets at the expense of the longer-term needs of patients and staff. The demand for fewer and less qualified staff to meet higher levels of clinical need has drastically reduced resources and opportunities for practitioners to think about the specific needs of individual clients, and has set too little value on processing and recovery time for staff and on the use of the expertise and creative capacity in properly maintained peer relationships and clinical teams.

Healthcare staff feel, in practical, intellectual and emotional ways, under-resourced, and reflective practice is often invoked as a way to bridge the gap. The problem here, of course, is that if the overall environment is in general terms not sufficiently supportive, reflective practice will unintentionally be set up to fail. A group of staff may recognise the need for time and space to process and make sense of clinical issues, but the system they are working within may operate in a way that runs counter to the aims and methods of reflective practice, and this tension may be difficult to reconcile.

The intense modern disillusionment with professionals and professional expertise, and the lack of trust which characterises the relationship between the professional and wider society, have also influenced the way in which practitioners approach reflective practice. Schon described the cause of these as the idealisation of professionalism and the unrealistic set of hopes and beliefs invested in professional training and expertise in Western society since the time of the Enlightenment. As he saw it, the educated ruling classes and professionals – and the science and technology upon which their activities were supposed to be based – came to be revered in much the same way as God had been in pre-Enlightenment times. The great, long moment of disillusionment in America was during the closing stages of the Vietnam war and the Watergate scandal, both of which exposed dishonesty and corruption at the highest levels of government. But if we look back at the last fifty years or so in the United States and the United Kingdom, this now looks like only the first of many such low periods.

Schon understood this disillusionment and distrust as partly the result of the improbable expectations placed on individual professional practitioners for so long. The over-investment in professional expertise in the Western world has led inevitably to disappointment, and sometimes even an attitude of contemptuous disregard. Reflective practice is presented by Schon as a corrective to the unrealistic amount of hope and belief invested in standard and purely technological solutions to human problems. In contrast with what he calls Technical Rationality, recognition of the uniqueness, complexity and ambiguity of the situations that face staff working to innovate and solve human problems is at the core of reflective practice.

One of the results of this disillusionment with professionals in the healthcare context is the top-down and bureaucratic management of risk and, as a consequence, widespread and pervasive defensive practice. Healthcare practitioners can feel as if they are under close, and even hostile, scrutiny and need to look after their own professional survival as a matter of priority, and an atmosphere prevails in many services in which anything a professional is unsure or worried about is covered up, rather than looked at and thought about. What seems to be lacking in many healthcare organisations is the capacity in both attitudes and procedures to distinguish between genuinely poor clinical practice, which does, of course, need to be identified and remedied, and the more normal ups and downs of the real-life work experience of most competent practitioners.

What this means is that those of us setting up and running reflective practice groups are working, to some extent at least, against the grain of modern healthcare systems. We operate in a context in which there is a high degree of ambivalence towards reflective practice, about which staff as individuals may not consciously be aware. On the one hand, colleagues recognise how crucial reflective practice is for staff well-being and the delivery of high-quality clinical care, and for the prevention of mistakes; but its development is frequently not supported, at least in any practical sense, at the service and organisational level. It can even be regarded as a threat, and actively opposed in some quarters, while being enthusiastically sought out in others.

For this reason, the model I present in this book has a strong systemic component. It emphasises the need for facilitators to take account of characteristics in the external environment in deciding whether to set up a reflective practice group, and to develop and maintain a feedback loop with managers and senior staff to ensure that ongoing consideration is given to what is needed for a reflective practice group to run properly.

The Intersubjective Model of Reflective Practice Groups and key influences

There are a number of models of reflective learning available, all of which describe a progression from a retrospective description of experience to its evaluation or analysis to learning output (Stedmon & Dallos, 2009). Borton's is simple and easy to use, with its three steps, each defined by a question: What? So What? And Now What? (Borton, 1970). Gibbs and Kolb both offer reflective learning cycles, which go from a retrospective review of experience to more active thinking about it, either through conceptual sense-making in Kolb's model or analytic work in Gibbs', to how to make use of this learning going forwards (Gibbs, 1998; Kolb, 2015). My model incorporates the notion of a reflective learning cycle but has been specifically developed for use in a group setting to facilitate thinking about practice in healthcare. It is a model with a particular context, which is an inter-subjective one: its focus is on developing relationships between health-care staff and their patients, and between colleagues in healthcare teams, and on building the resource provided by a group of colleagues to improve practice and well-being at work.

The Intersubjective Model of Reflective Practice Groups describes a series of stages which are, to my mind, the key ingredients of this way of thinking about clinical work. The order of the stages, which is shown in the diagram on page 10, represents the structure or flow of a reflective practice session. In reality, groups will not always attend to each activity in every session, or will give more emphasis to one activity over another at a particular stage in the life of the group.

The stages are as follows: contracting and regular review, both within the reflective practice group and with senior staff in the orga-nisation; some form of transition from busy, pressured healthcare environments to the reflective mode; space to follow up on thoughts stimulated by previous sessions, charting developments in thinking in the group across time; the generation of material from practice by one member of the group for other members to reflect on; a stage of free responding, in which immediate and intuitive feelings and reactions to the material are acknowledged and looked at; a stage of more effortful thinking, in which the group steps back and tries to give meaning to what has been presented, building a more processed account of what is going on; and lastly, discussion of how to apply the thinking of the group in the external situation, acknowledging real-world constraints and the need for flexibility in bringing together theory and practice.

The aim of the model is to create a supportive and effective group resource for thinking about the problems, challenges and dilemmas we all face in our clinical work. Its focus is often on relationships; and its medium, the way in which it produces learning about practice, is through the meeting of minds, or intersubjectivities. The model starts with the subjective experience of a single group member, and the invitation for them to add to the conventional clinical descriptions, with which we are so familiar, detail about the client as a three-dimensional person, and about the client's interactions and relationships, including the relationship with the presenting practitioner. The model then uses relationships in the group and engagement with the material by the other group members to open up thinking about practice. This is not at all the same as one-to-one supervision, in that the medium of the Intersubjective Model is the relationships in the group, which the facilitator aims to foster as a valuable and creative peer resource.

There are three main influences on the type of reflective practice outlined in the Intersubjective Model, which are explored in more detail in the Key Influences sections of chapters describing the various stages. The model represents a hybrid approach, drawing on the experiential learning, phenomenological and psychoanalytic traditions of thought and practice. It has been shaped by the tradition of experiential learning and critical thinking that grew out of twentieth-century educational philosophy, and which lies behind Schon's concept of the reflective practitioner. It has also been influenced, through my experience as a qualitative researcher, by phenomenological theory, in which all knowledge begins with individual sensation and perception, and in which there is always a relationship between a subject and an object that together make up a subjective field. This, the subjective experience of the working life of a colleague, is where we start from in a reflective practice group, moving outwards to take in and make use of the reactions of others. The model draws very much, too, on psychoanalytic thinking about the clinical value of working with emotion in the room, and of developing an understanding of relational processes and the power and possibility of unconscious communication. Its focus is on helping practitioners become aware of what is going on in therapeutic and helping relationships, and it does this by encouraging practitioners' interest in their interactions with clients and in their emotional and intuitive sense of what is happening.

The group element expresses a commitment to collegiate values, including a belief in the importance of being able to draw on fellow practitioners for help, support and guidance. The aim in the Intersubjective Model of drawing on and building up the resources of a group of healthcare staff is rooted in a collectivist vision, in which clinical work at ground level is held and sustained by a strong healthcare community.

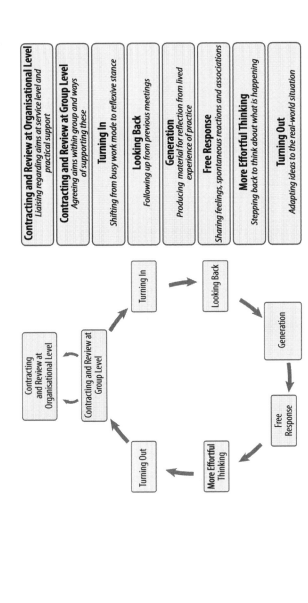

Contracting and Review at Organisational Level
Liaising regarding aims at service level and practical support

Contracting and Review at Group Level
Agreeing aims within group and ways of supporting these

Turning In
Shifting from busy work mode to reflexive stance

Looking Back
Following up from previous meetings

Generation
Producing material for reflection from lived experience of practice

Free Response
Sharing feelings, spontaneous reactions and associations

More Effortful Thinking
Stepping back to think about what is happening

Turning Out
Adapting ideas to the real-world situation

Contracting and Review at Organisational Level

Contracting and Review at Group Level

Turning In

Looking Back

Generation

Free Response

More Effortful Thinking

Turning Out

Figure 1.1 Diagram of the Intersubjective Model of Reflective Practice Groups

Why this book?

When I started to deliver reflective practice training, I was struck by the fact that experienced colleagues talked about feeling at sea with the facilitation of reflective practice groups. There was this repeated question: what exactly is reflective practice? Everybody was talking about it and agreed that it was useful and important. But it was very difficult to say precisely what it was. There seemed to exist a widespread assumption that reflective practice was a relatively straightforward activity and something which practitioners should already know about and know how to do. The reality was an entirely different one. The facilitation of reflective practice groups did not appear easy or straightforward to colleagues at all, particularly when they started to actually run groups.

At this point, colleagues were often met with a confusing mixture of responses. This would typically entail an enthusiastic first invitation from a manager or senior member of staff to provide reflective practice, followed by all sorts of problems once the colleague began to attempt to make concrete arrangements for the group to start. Staff could not find the time to come to a group, or failed to turn up once a group was set up, or could only find a place to meet that was more like a thoroughfare than a private room for thinking about confidential material. These experiences of organisational ambivalence could lead to facilitators feeling isolated, confused and inadequate. They sometimes described what is known as imposter syndrome, the sense that others knew all about what reflective practice was and how to go about doing it successfully, and they ought to know about it as well but felt they did not. They asked for me to produce a model to help them, and they seemed to find it helpful when I shared my approach to reflective practice.

Originally the Intersubjective Model was an attempt to be explicit in describing my best work as a facilitator of reflective practice groups: by this, I mean that it contains within it, in the form of a series of stages to a group meeting, the key constituent ingredients of reflective practice as I might do it on a good day or over a series of meetings. In the past, I rarely covered all the stages of the model in a single group meeting, although I do that more often now, because I have been influenced by the construction of the model. This book presents the model and is firmly intended as a guide to practice, helping practitioners to develop and extend their own individual approach to the facilitation of reflective practice groups, rather than prescribing a fixed, concrete approach.

Who is this book for and how should it be used?

The Intersubjective Model for Reflective Practice Groups can be applied across a range of healthcare settings in both mental and physical health services. It has been developed for staff working with any healthcare population for whom it would be helpful to widen and deepen thinking about difficulties, and particularly, to develop an awareness of the interactions involved in the clinical encounter and the impact of work on staff. It is hard to think of a healthcare population for whom it would not potentially be of relevance.

Much of my experience in facilitating reflective practice groups have been with clinical psychologists. I have coordinated the reflective practice seminar programme on the Leicester clinical psychology training course for the past seventeen years. This programme consists of six reflective practice groups for trainees, two groups of six to eight per cohort, each of which is facilitated by a pair of clinical psychologists across the three years of training. I have co-facilitated six of these groups myself. As part of this role, I have organised annual reviews when facilitators across the programme come together to share experiences of running the groups. These reviews also provide a useful opportunity to troubleshoot with fellow-facilitators as and when problems emerge.

I have also facilitated reflective practice groups for nurses, probation officers and multidisciplinary mental health colleagues over the years; and in addition, nurses, social workers, occupational therapists and healthcare managers have attended recent training courses I have delivered on how to run reflective practice groups. My view is that reflective practice may vary in its style and emphasis depending on professional discipline, but healthcare staff from across disciplines are able to facilitate and make use of reflective practice groups. It is my firm intention for the Intersubjective Model to be used by all healthcare professions: that is, by nurses, social workers, physicians and psychiatrists, clinical psychologists, occupational therapists and art and music therapists. I hope too that managers and others involved in designing and developing healthcare services will engage with it. For this reason, each stage of the model describes an activity, which is applicable across disciplines and specific schools of therapy or clinical practice. I have tried to write in a jargon-free way in outlining the model so that the essentials of each stage come across to the reader and can then be used to inform specific, more localised procedures and modes of practice.

Who is able to facilitate a reflective practice group? Healthcare colleagues are in the position to do this if they have a reasonable amount of clinical experience, some familiarity with and a feel for work in groups and teams, and a positive and informed attitude to reflective supervision. There is plenty of room for flexibility here; interest in and keenness to engage in reflective practice are probably more important than concrete experience and training. But experience does make a difference. I have found that those who themselves have had a reasonably good, safe experience of a reflective practice group feel much more able to facilitate one themselves. I have also learned that it is more common than we would wish for colleagues to have had negative and unsafe experiences of reflective practice, and it is important to process these in preparing a practitioner to go on to offer a group themselves.

Clinical or practice experience is a first important prerequisite because of the professional credibility needed to run a group for staff aimed at developing high-level thinking in response to clinical problems and challenges. It is not, for a moment, that the facilitator needs to have answers to everything. But it helps enormously if they have been tried and tested clinically, and have developed a certain robustness in the face of pressures and difficulties. The potential reflective practice group facilitator should also have had some experience of working with groups and teams, even if they have not directly facilitated groups before, so that they feel confident and able to function in a group setting. Some experience of being in the supervisor role is useful as well. It can be intimidating to lead what is, in essence, a form of supervision group for colleagues if one has not had experience of providing supervision in other, perhaps more straightforwardly hierarchical, settings. In addition, it is helpful to have received training in supervisory practice. Short courses to develop and support supervisors are widely available these days, helping staff make the transition from learner to a position of responsibility for the learning of others.

Last but not least, the facilitator of a reflective practice group should have access to their own ongoing supervision and support. Group facilitation of this kind is complex and sometimes lonely work, which involves attending to different levels of process and activity in the group and, sometimes, being on the receiving end of powerful group dynamics. It is helpful to have a space for digestion of what is going on, either with a supervisor or a group of peers, and to receive support and guidance. This may be provided by a fellow facilitator rather than a supervisor. On the Leicester training course, all our groups are facilitated in pairs, and this is regarded very positively. In a National Health Service Trust to which I have delivered training, a network of peers involved in the facilitation of reflective practice groups has been set up. They have organised an email discussion group and meet, not often but regularly, to sustain and support one other.

Organisation of the book

The book consists of eight chapters, which offer descriptions of the eight stages of the model, followed by a Conclusion in which I reflect on what I have learned through the process of researching and writing. Each chapter starts with a broad definition of what the stage is about and how, as a facilitator, to approach it. A more detailed discussion of critical issues follows, outlining the sorts of dilemmas and problems that facilitators are likely to encounter at each stage. There is then a full illustration from practice or, in relation to the Looking Back stage, from research into practice. These mainly come from my own work as a facilitator of reflective practice groups; but I was keen to feature at least one example of a reflective practice group for nurses, and so in the chapter on the More Effortful Thinking stage, I have drawn on the work of a colleague. The illustrations sometimes show how to facilitate a group at a particular stage, and sometimes they exemplify a real-life and realistically imperfect approach to a common problem. The facilitation of reflective practice groups is often more about enabling engagement with the messiness and complexity of clinical practice than about performing or being too focused on a right way of doing things, and I wanted to show this in the examples I used. A section on techniques follows in most of the chapters. This section does not by any means provide an exhaustive list of possible techniques; instead, it offers some ideas about the ways in which different facilitators have approached the stage in question. Lastly, there is a section on key influences; this presents the reader with the ideas from theory and the empirical research, which has informed the development of my thinking at each stage. This section can be omitted by those who are interested in the model from a purely practical point of view, but it will, I hope, be useful for those who like to make links between theory and practice.

This book is intended as a guide to practice, and the experience of reading it is meant to be as much like attending a live, interactive training event as possible. I have tried to write it in a clear, accessible way, keeping the needs of the practitioner in mind, and to give plenty of examples so the reader builds a full and realistic picture of reflective practice on the ground.

I recommend that the reader with limited time gives priority to Chapters 2, 4, 5 and 6. The focus on Contracting and Review at the Organisational Level in Chapter 2 is a distinct feature of the model, offering, in my view, much-needed recognition of the role of the work environment, supportive or otherwise, in the success of a reflective practice group. The three central chapters, which describe the stages of the Generation of material, Free Responding to it and then More Effortful Thinking, are at the core of the model. These three stages work in concert to produce the essentials of what I think of as group reflective practice in a healthcare setting: the engagement of the creative, emotional and intellectual resources of a group of individuals with diverse perspectives and talents to develop an in-depth and relational understanding of the unique and complex human situations faced by professionals in clinical practice.

References

Aesop (this edition 1998) *Aesop The complete fables.* London: Penguin Classics.

Bambling, M., King, R., Raue, P., Schweitzer, R. & Lambert, W. (2006) Clinical supervision: its influence on client-rated working alliance and client symptom reduction in the brief treatment of major depression. *Psychotherapy Research*, 16(3): 317–331.

Berg, A., Hansson, U.W. & Hallberg, I.R. (1994) Nurses' creativity, tedium and burnout during 1 year of clinical supervision and implementation of individually planned nursing care: comparison between a ward for severely demented patients and a similar control ward. *Journal of Advanced Nursing*, 20(4): 742–749.

Borton, T. (1970) *Reach, touch and teach: student concerns and process education.* New York: McGraw-Hill Education.

Bradshaw, T., Butterworth, A. & Mairs, H. (2007) Does structured clinical supervision during psychosocial intervention education enhance outcome for mental health nurses and the service users they work with? *Journal of Psychiatric and Mental Health Nursing*, 14(1): 4–12.

Dewey, J. (this edition 1997, first published 1910) *How we think.* New York: Dover Publications, Inc.

Edmondson, A.C. & Verdin, P.V. (2018) The strategic imperative of psychological safety and organizational error management. In Hagen, J.U. (Ed.) *How could this happen? Managing errors in organizations.* Cham, Switzerland: Palgrave Macmillan.

Edwards, D., Burnard, P., Hannigan, B., Cooper, L., Adams, J., Juggesur, T., Fothergill, A. & Coyle, D. (2006) Clinical supervision and burnout: the influence of clinical supervision for community mental health nurses. *Journal of Clinical Nursing*, 15(8): 1007–1015.

Esterhuizen, P., & Howatson-Jones, L. (2019) *Reflective practice in nursing* (4th ed.). Thousand Oaks, California: Sage Publications Inc.

Gibbs, G. (1998) *Learning by doing: a guide to teaching and learning methods.* Oxford: Further Education Unit, Oxford Polytechnic UK.

Hall, L.H., Johnson, J., Watt, I., Tsipa, A. & O'Connor, D.B. (2016) Healthcare staff wellbeing, burnout and patient safety: a systematic review. *PLOS One*, 11(7): e015905. doi:10.1371/journal.pone.0159015.

Hyrkas, K. (2005) Clinical supervision, burnout and job satisfaction among mental health and psychiatric nurses in Finland. *Issues in Mental Health Nursing*, 26(5): 531–556.

Kolb, D.A. (2015, first published in 1984) *Experiential learning: experience as the source of learning and development* (2nd ed.). New Jersey, NJ: Pearson Education, Inc.

Lavender, T. (2003) Redressing the balance: the place, history and future of reflective practice in clinical psychology training. *Clinical Psychology Forum*, 27: 11–15. Leicester: The British Psychological Society.

Schon, D.A. (1983) *The reflective practitioner: how professionals think in action.* Farnham, Surrey: Ashgate Books Ltd.

Stedmon, J. & Dallos, R. (Eds.) (2009) *Reflective practice in psychotherapy and counselling.* Maidenhead, Berkshire: Open University Press.

White, E. & Winstanley, J. (2010) A randomised controlled trial of clinical supervision: selected findings from a novel Australian attempt to establish the evidence base for causal relationships with quality of care and patient outcomes, as an informed contribution to mental health nursing practice development. *Journal of Research in Nursing*, 15(2): 151–167.

2 Contracting and Review at the Organisational Level

What is Contracting and Review at the Organisational Level?

Clinical colleagues have repeated the same story of bewilderment and frustration to me time and again: they are asked, even pleaded with, to offer a reflective practice group and told of how long staff have waited for such a resource and of how helpful it will be to staff who have no space to think; once they have agreed to the request and start trying to facilitate a group they are met with all sorts of unexpected obstacles, such as difficulties with finding a room or staff saying they are too busy to attend or can only come sporadically. The stories differ in their particulars, but the theme is the same: reflective practice in the abstract is a very good thing, but when it comes down to it, it is not supported in practical and operational terms at the organisational level. Staff who are invited to facilitate reflective practice groups have a contradictory experience, meeting a positive response in some quarters and a neutral or negative one in others. And too often committed colleagues continue to offer reflective practice groups in environments which do not appear to support the work they are doing, struggling on in isolation and unsure at times of whether working against the grain of the organisation in this way is ultimately helpful for the staff or not.

In recognition of the ubiquity of these difficulties, Contracting and Review at the Organisational Level has become a foundational stage of the Intersubjective Model. It is helpful to draw on organisational theory in order to better understand the apparent paradox whereby, on the one hand, reflective practice is much sought after and widely regarded as integral to the provision of a quality clinical service, and on the other hand, it often seems impossible to take fairly simple steps to set it up in a sustainable way. The aim of this stage is three-fold: to help groups run more smoothly by opening up a channel of communication with managers and, where possible, by ensuring their

buy-in and support; to develop reflective cultures in healthcare organisations, educating staff at the most senior level as to the value and
importance of a thoughtful, emotionally in-touch and creative
approach towards the complexities of clinical work, both to the
delivery of a high-quality clinical service and to the growth over time
of a non-defensive environment, in which staff are to learn from
mistakes and improve their practice accordingly; and last but not
least, to assist staff in making decisions about when management
support is insufficient and the work should not go ahead – at least,
not for the time being.

Organisational contracting and review involves initial discussion
with managers or senior staff about a request to set up a reflective
practice group, the purpose of such a group, the practical and organisational support needed to make it work and development of a plan for
ongoing feedback. These communications can be fairly minimal, and
certainly any feedback to senior staff about what is going on in a
reflective practice group should be both general and anonymous,
describing overall themes in group discussions rather than the details
of cases or the opinions and reactions of individual group members.

For example, at the six-month review point, the group might identify
two or three topics that have emerged from discussions to put in a brief
summary report for managers. This would not include details, which
allowed any individual, either a client or a member of the group, to be
identified. Managers rarely need to know about the specific content of
what is spoken about in reflective practice. But it is useful to give them
a sense of the staff's experiences of the work environment and to open
up a line of communication so that managers are involved in, rather
than excluded from, reflective practice in their service, and can offer
help and support if necessary. In addition, regular feedback is a useful
way of educating senior staff about reflective practice if they do not
know about it already: what reflective practice is and what it is not,
what sort of impact it can have on staff well-being and relationships
and on clinical outcomes, and the overall culture of service.

One of the reasons it makes such good sense to involve senior staff
in contractual and review activity in this way is because problems in
setting up and maintaining reflective practice groups so often result
from a lack of coordination between practitioners on the ground and
managers 'up above'. It is always worth asking what outcome managers would expect or like to see from the introduction of a reflective
practice group. This may or may not be different from what practitioners on the ground want to get out of it. If agendas diverge, it is
helpful to iron out these differences as early as possible, or at least for

the facilitator to be aware of them to avoid the group being under-mined further down the line. It may be that the group is able to incor-porate a managerial viewpoint into its discussions at the contractual stage about what practitioners want to get from the group, making room for both perspectives, even in small ways. For example, practi-tioners may want to focus on clinical issues in reflective practice, whereas managers may be concerned about high levels of sickness absence amongst staff. The group may then give more attention in its feedback to managers to the impact of certain aspects of the work situation on staff, suggesting how reflective practice helps in reducing stress and burnout, and the ways in which other aspects of the envir-onment need to change for sickness levels to go down.

In matters of business, the advice is to carry out significant negotia-tions before a contract is signed, at the point of maximum leverage. Similarly, when preparing to facilitate a reflective practice group, it is best not to rush into things and make demands for increased resources, or to ask for changes in arrangements before starting the group, when there is still a question as to whether it can or should go ahead. All too often, a facilitator will agree to offer a group without specifying the necessary resources. This is the point at which to say that you need a regular, private space in order to run a group so when you start you do not find yourself in a communal space such as a kitchen with people walking in and out.

Sometimes, problems of organisational support result from a rela-tively straightforward lack of knowledge and understanding about reflective practice. But sometimes the problem is a deeper one of orga-nisational ambivalence towards reflective practice or the reflective stance – or even frank hostility. The problems colleagues report in attempting to provide reflective practice groups are many and varied. What they have in common is the feeling they produce in the facilitator of being irrelevant and unimportant, compared with the significance attributed to what is perceived as the 'real work' of responding to clinical demands. Studies of prison and forensic settings have observed the way in which the reflective or psychotherapeutic stance can be dis-missed as soft and ineffective, in contrast with the hard realism of staff who are involved day-in-day-out with the practicalities of care and control (Hinshelwood, 1993; Kurtz, 2002).

Organisational obstructions to setting up reflective practice groups tend also to strike facilitators as having a 'given' quality to them, as if whatever problem they are encountering – whether it is to do with the lack of an available room or shift patterns on the ward or relentless work pressures – is an aspect of how things are in the organisation and simply cannot be questioned. My advice would be to remain curious, inwardly if not outwardly, about the fact that these difficulties are communicated as being beyond question.

The 'given' quality to these aspects of organisational character and function should help us recognise them as part of what Isabel Menzies Lyth described in the 1960s as a 'social defence system' (Menzies Lyth, 1960). This refers to the ways that over time groups and organisations develop counter-productive practices to defend against aspects of the work task, which are felt to be too difficult to face. An example from Menzies Lyth's pioneering study of nursing service in a general hospital was the division of nursing tasks according to specific jobs, which were carried out across patients, rather than for individuals. Nurses referred to diseased body parts or illnesses and not to patients: for example, they spoke of 'the liver in bed 10' or 'the pneumonia in bed 15'. This meant that nurses spent little time with any one patient and could not really get to know the people they cared for as relatable human beings. Menzies Lyth understood this work pattern as defensive, since it functioned to reduce possibilities for engagement with patients, and, therefore, distanced staff from the reality of their pain and suffering.

Social defences are different from defences in individuals or groups that have recently formed; these defences tend to feel 'hotter', taking us close to a painful or sensitive area. By contrast, social defences become institutionalised, often presenting as common-sense aspects of custom and practice. It is only when we stand back that questions start to occur. Surely it is counter-therapeutic for staff and patients to have so little opportunity to get to know each other as fellow human beings? Surely it is unhelpful for staff activities to be monitored and controlled to such an extent that they are too busy to stop and think? Will they not make more mistakes that way and become less efficient? Is something being avoided in a service in which shift patterns are organised so that nursing staff never have time to come together and discuss things as a whole group?

The theory of social defence systems suggests that the practitioner who is trying to bring about any sort of change with individuals in an organisation where there are strong defences at play should operate at two levels. They should address the underlying anxieties of staff, which led to the formation of the defensive system, and, at the same time, they should modify the system to enable it to contain these anxieties in a more productive way. Working at one of these levels without taking account of the other is potentially counter-productive, because it risks either taking down defensive practices, which have developed for good reason, without tending to their underlying causes; or it risks opening up areas of feeling and experience for which organisational structures and supports simply do not have a place.

What this means is that if facilitators of a reflective practice group do not at least bear in mind the organisational context, the staff may connect with aspects of their working experience, such as the feelings evoked by clients and the challenges of the clinical task, for which there is no space or support at the service level. For example, if the staff within a service are only allowed to see clients six times and there is no room for negotiation on this, it is going to be difficult if reflective practice encourages them to engage with their clinical work in a deeper and more empathic way. This may bring real clinical and professional gains, influencing the way they understand their interactions with patients and helping them reconnect with why they chose to do the work they do. But the conflict it produces between what is desirable and what is possible does at least need to be acknowledged. It is also empowering for staff to find some way of communicating this tension to managers, creating the possibility that reflective practice can lead to changes at the cultural level of the organisation.

Just as Freud began by seeing transference reactions during therapy as an obstruction, but ended up regarding them as a primary focus for therapeutic work, I would like organisational responses to reflective practice and the question of organisational support to be a cornerstone of the Intersubjective Model. My hope is that by incorporating organisational ambivalence into the model, by recognising how common it is and offering a way to begin to address it, problems that have been regarded as getting in the way of reflective practice will start to be seen as grist to its mill. Some work at addressing systemic ambivalence and facilitating reflective practice at the service level should become part of what we are trying to do, rather than an irritating side issue.

Critical issues from practice

A common problem is for the organisational dimension – and particularly the attitude of stakeholders and senior staff towards reflective practice and what they might want from it – to be missed by the group, certainly in terms of the way the group defines its purpose and sets itself up. The management agenda often then rears its head in the form of an ongoing complaint by group members, sometimes a grievous one, but not something about which the group feels it can, or even should, do anything.

Table 2.1 Activities and aims at the organisational stage of contracting

Activity at the organisational level	Aim of activity
Contact managers/senior staff to inform them of the request, and suggest a meeting to discuss it	Open up a line of communication with the aim of getting buy-in and support
If possible, meet to discuss the request and what you anticipate offering; if it is not possible to do this face-to-face, do it by telephone or email	Promote understanding of reflective practice and what it has to offer; gain an understanding of desired outcomes from a managerial point of view
As part of this discussion, consider the question of what you need to run a group properly (see the following section for more on this)	See if it is possible to negotiate decent practical support for the group before you start, such as the use of a room away from the day-to-day work environment or a change in shift patterns to enable the staff to attend regularly
If basic requirements are not met, consider whether to proceed with the group or not	Avoid a situation in which you press ahead and offer a group without basic organisational support
Provide feedback at review points, say six-monthly or at least annually	Demystify reflective practice; let managers know about ground-level experiences; where possible, take account of both staff and management agendas; develop reflective culture and support for reflective practice group

I think of the role of the facilitator at the contractual stage as having both outward and inward-facing aspects to it, rather like Rice's description in social systems theory of how a manager should position themselves at the boundary of the organisation, aiming to remain in touch with the concerns of ground-level staff but aware also of the broader picture, the context in which the work takes place and which gives it wider relevance and meaning (Rice, 1969). The task of the facilitator is both to help the group define its own internal sense of purpose and to reconcile this – or at least bring it into as constructive a relationship as possible – with the demands of the external environment. The objective here is not to reconcile the irreconcilable; instead, it is to bring the perspectives of staff and managers regarding the way clinical work is thought about and carried out into some sort of ongoing relationship, rather than going along with the illusion that the two groups exist in two separate worlds.

As an example, I facilitated a supervision group for clinical psychologists offering weekly reflective practice to groups of staff in the Community Mental Health Teams in which they worked. The clinical psychologists felt that the overall agenda of the employing mental health trust was at odds with their aims as experienced clinicians and supervisors. The trust was seen to be preoccupied with efficiency ratings and financial targets, over and above the quality of clinical care and long-term outcomes for clients. My colleagues' facilitation of reflective practice groups was the focus of our discussions. However, we were intrigued to notice that these groups seemed to have an impact on the way staff managed their caseloads. Staff reported discharging more clients than before and taking on more new assessments. The groups appeared to offer the support and confidence staff needed to discharge patients they had felt stuck with, sometimes for years, and to take on the challenge of new work. Reflective practice, which can be seen by managers as not having to do with efficiency, was having a marked, positive influence on throughput. We did not bring this discovery to the attention of senior staff in the organisation at the time. But in retrospect, we should certainly have done so.

Sometimes, the facilitator will be able to liaise with senior staff during the contractual stage whilst also maintaining a focus on the needs of group members. But if the staff and management agendas of the organisation are far apart from each other, it may work better to separate the inward- and outward-facing roles, and for someone other than the facilitator to arrange practical support and keep open a line of communication with senior staff. I have worked with colleagues facilitating reflective practice groups who have formed peer support networks. These are a useful resource for swapping facilitators across services so they are not offering groups to staff in their own clinical teams, or for dividing up the tasks of facilitation and organisational liaison across groups.

It can happen that concerns about what is going on in the wider organisation threaten to take over a group, leaving little room for the consideration of clinical practice. Groups can become overly focused on organisational issues, and facilitators report feeling unsure of what to do about this. On the one hand, the experiences of staff within underfunded public healthcare organisations are frequently very difficult indeed, and it only seems right that staff should have a space to process them. On the other hand, groups can get stuck in a complaining mode, increasingly demoralised by problems in the external environment which threaten to compromise the care they are able to offer, and about which it seems as if nothing can be done.

If the situation within the organisation is a particularly challenging one, and the safety of staff or patients is at risk, I think the facilitator has a duty to take this up at a senior level, preferably with the cooperation, and always with the knowledge, of the group. For example, if, as a facilitator, you hear about low levels of staffing and frequent episodes of violence on a ward, and the situation seems unsafe, it is important for the group to raise this as an issue with managers. Hopefully, concerns can be lodged with someone who has the power to address them, enabling the group to restore its focus on ground-level practice.

There is a balance to be struck here between giving space for staff to consider the organisational issues that frame their clinical work and capacity to function as practitioners, and colluding with a defensive preoccupation with external issues. It can be much easier for a group of clinicians to join together in looking at what is happening externally than to look inwards at their own practice, and the differences of viewpoint and opinion between various group members. Sometimes, facilitators need to be firm in getting the group to do this. It is best if facilitators are flexible enough to allow some space to hear about organisational concerns and learn about the impact of these on staff, but manage to retain a focus on ground-level practice. In keeping this emphasis, the facilitator of a reflective practice group holds onto the value of thoughtful, high-quality clinical care, and restores and develops the sense of rightful pride the staff take in their work.

A third common problem is when facilitators put up with a complete lack of basic support and infrastructure for a reflective practice group, rather than addressing these environmental inadequacies directly – either by working to improve matters or by deciding that the group cannot go ahead. Contracting for, and reviewing the running of, a group at the organisational level should open a dialogue with service heads about what is needed to facilitate a group. Hopefully, this will result in the provision of basic resources and support, such as the use of a private room and the arrangement of rotas and timetables which allow staff to attend regularly, or if not regularly then predictably. But this may not be the case. I have often heard from colleagues who have carried on trying to facilitate a reflective practice group in the most unpromising conditions. Should they have done this? Is it a good idea to continue to give up to a half-day each fortnight to a staff group who can only meet for half an hour in a crowded office with interruptions, or who can attend so infrequently that on many occasions there are only one or two staff members there?

I think there is a judgement call to be made on whether to offer a group in very difficult circumstances, and we should be more willing to make the decision not to offer, or continue to offer, a reflective practice group if basic conditions are not met. It seems important to be flexible and to work patiently with staff teams to try to improve conditions, but also to avoid the demoralising and wasteful situation in which a skilled and experienced practitioner turns up week after week to a chaotic and disordered setting, in which the staff are unable to make use of what is on offer. Sometimes colleagues in such situations have described feeling that in the service they and they alone hold onto a belief in the value of reflective practice. They have found themselves, for example, sending emails out each week before a group to drum up attendance. This may be a helpful mode of operation at a particular stage in the life of a group, but it should not persist. It is not up to the facilitator, and only to the facilitator, to make a reflective practice group work. Indeed, such a venture cannot succeed if the facilitator is left carrying all the motivation and energy for the group as a whole.

Illustration: I embark on reflective practice training without sufficient understanding of who commissioned it and why

I was invited to deliver a two-day training course on how to run reflective practice groups for a large healthcare trust in the National Health Service. Initially I was approached by a clinical psychology colleague working in this trust. His post involved the provision of psychology services to five in-patient psychiatric wards in a general hospital setting. He felt he was spread very thinly across the five wards, certainly in terms of the number of individual patients he could see, and he had the idea of offering reflective practice groups as a resource for the staff on the wards. He could facilitate a few such groups and provide something for each ward that way. He knew of colleagues who were interested in a similar plan and thought that they might be able to group together to get funding for some training from me.

It was a while before I heard again about the proposed training, and when I did it was from a woman who was working in the educational department of the trust. She had spoken to the clinical psychologist working on the wards, and had decided to initiate a trust-wide development, providing reflective practice training and ongoing support to around fifty staff, all of whom would commit to running at least one reflective practice group in different parts of the service. She was enthusiastic about this idea, and I was pleased to be a part of what sounded like an innovative and worthwhile project.

On the first day of the course I arrived at a training venue, which was in a separate location from the main clinical and administrative buildings where trust staff worked. There were a couple of technical support staff on-site, and they were very helpful. However, there was no one from clinical services or the educational department to meet with me or discuss the overall plan for the training. I suddenly felt very much on my own with the task of engaging with a large group of staff from an unfamiliar organisation with little contextual information. As I started to talk in front of the group I was struck by their mixed responses. Usually the healthcare colleagues that attend my courses are in favour of reflective practice: it is something they believe in, and they are keen to think about what it is and how to develop it. On this occasion some of the people in the room engaged positively in this way; but quite a few others were clearly not interested, talking amongst themselves and looking at their phones. Then someone asked about what sort of support was going to be offered after the end of the training, and someone else made a comment about how it was all very well having this one-off training but what was going to happen afterwards? I realised that attendees were talking to me as if I was a representative of the trust, even a member of staff working in it, rather than an external person who had been invited to provide a specific bit of training which fitted into a larger project.

During the course of the day some questions began to form in my mind. I wondered what the staff had been told about the overall project, and how the staff had been selected to attend the training. I wondered who was there from choice and who had been told by their manager to attend. I found I had only a hazy memory of the plan to support the development of reflective practice in the trust going forwards, and it seemed unclear whether such a plan still existed, and if it did exist, who was leading on it. It felt as if the training I was delivering had no context, making it difficult for those attending to think about how they might apply their learning.

I spoke to attendees about this the following day. Most were unable to say who was leading on the project and were unaware of any plan for ongoing training and support. Some had volunteered to come because reflective practice was an area of interest; others were there because they had been instructed to attend by their manager. It was helpful for all of us to reflect on how the lack of a clear sense of how the training fitted into the organisational agenda had affected us, and this was particularly the case for those who had simply been told to come without having a sense of the broader picture. This discussion led to a much more positive atmosphere on the second day of the course.

Table 2.2 Guidelines for making the decision as to whether conditions are good enough to go ahead with facilitating a group

Common issues	How to determine whether to go ahead or not
Low or sporadic attendance by staff	Is there real commitment amongst some (a minimum of three – the smallest number for a group) staff or not? Determine whether problems in attendance result from genuine difficulties in work structures and organisation (e.g. nursing rotas, which might be changed over time) or deeper ambivalence
Lack of provision of a private, uninterrupted space to meet	Groups can make do with rooms which are uncomfortable and even with meeting in different places (although comfort and stability are both important), but they must at least have regular access to a private space
Lack of available protected time	An hour is the minimum for a monthly group; if it is possible to meet more frequently, 45 minutes might be possible
Ethos in external environment experienced by staff as unsupportive of and/ or contradictory to reflective practice	This is a matter of degree: it is common for staff to experience tension, but if over time it seems impossible to make use of the work of the group, even in small ways, it may be too frustrating to continue

We learnt that the psychologist who had originally contacted me had spoken with a senior colleague in the trust, who had then liaised with the educational department to develop the project. Things were more joined up than they had initially appeared to be, and it was useful to have a better idea of who might be leading the development and thinking about support for it in the future.

After the course finished, I exchanged emails with the senior colleague and with the staff in the educational department. We made a plan for me to deliver a second training course, and for this to be introduced at the start of the day by the senior colleague so those attending understood something of the history of the project, and what might be available for them in terms of support going forwards. We talked about what type of future support would be needed. I suggested they appoint someone experienced from amongst the group of staff facilitating reflective practice groups to join with them in coordinating the project. I felt it was important for those in charge to have regular contact with someone doing the work on the ground. By the time I delivered my second course, this person had been appointed and had started to form a network of facilitators. There was a much greater sense amongst those attending of support in the organisation for the development of reflective practice.

It is useful to draw a couple of learning points from this experience. I was confused by the fact that different people had been in touch with me to set up the work, and chose not to ask questions, probably for fear of appearing stupid. In future, if invited to offer training or facilitate a group for an outside organisation, I will take more care to piece together an understanding of who is commissioning the work and why, and not be afraid to ask naïve questions about the roles and relationships of people within an unfamiliar service. When I have understood something of the commissioning context, I will think about who would be best placed to deliver information to participants. It is helpful if a manager is willing to meet with staff to give a rationale for any development, rather than leaving the trainer or facilitator to carry this responsibility. I will also try to avoid making the assumption that organisational support is lacking. This experience has taught me that it may feel this way because of how disconnected the different groups of staff in large and complex healthcare organisations can be. But sometimes support and interest are readily available if one finds out a bit more about how an organisation operates, and works actively with people at this more systemic level.

Key influences

The model of the social defence system developed by Isabel Menzies Lyth and Elliott Jacques in the 1950s has had a formative effect on my thinking about organisational life (Jacques, 1955; Menzies Lyth, 1960). In developing reflective practice, it has helped me understand the mixed and contradictory organisational responses so often encountered by colleagues towards reflective practice groups, and convinced me of the value of including an organisational stage to the process of contracting and review. There is a small but growing body of research pointing towards the role that environmental support plays in making the difference between whether clinical supervision is effective or not. This has strengthened my view that work at the systemic level is vital to the development of reflective practice in healthcare, and that the question of whether there is adequate support at the service level is a valid one in considering whether to facilitate a group.

The social defence paradigm provides a way of understanding the paradoxical way in which reflective practice, which promotes explorative thinking about the clinical task and by extension the work of the organisation, is often seen as a good thing at the same time as being actively marginalised and resisted. Menzies Lyth and Jacques were both concerned with understanding the reasons why defensive practices developed at the social or organisational level. Jacques focused his explanation on the way in which defences in the overall culture of an organisation develop in response to the needs of individual members, so that the organisation comes to function as a container for these. By contrast Menzies Lyth concentrated on the way defences build in order to cope with the anxieties generated by the working task of the organisation, paying particular attention to the emotions produced by the job of caring for the vulnerable and the sick.

In her writing Menzies Lyth brings to life the primitive anxieties evoked by the power and responsibility invested in the clinical role. These anxieties relate both to our capacity for creativity and care, and also to the limits of our resources and the understandable feelings of irritation and frustration that exist to a greater or lesser extent in all of us. This aspect of her work makes a great deal of sense to healthcare workers; it helps them to get in touch with their desire to heal others and do good in the world, and the way in which this can tip into an unrealistic wish to make everything better. And, conversely, it can enable staff to be honest about their more destructive urges, and their frustrations and feelings of being overwhelmed by the nature of their task. Reflective practice offers a space in which staff are invited to open up about these feelings, and it makes complete sense that at a system-wide level this provokes the social defences which originally developed in order to cope with them.

At a conference at Oxford University in 2013 the social defence paradigm was revisited in the light of developments in psychoanalytic theory and social and political life, such as the emergence of the global market economy (Armstrong & Rustin, 2015). The papers presented have an interesting new emphasis on the reciprocity of psychological and social forces, and the way, for example, healthcare services in the UK National Health Service (NHS) are influenced, not just by the experiences of staff in relation to the task of caring for patients, but by pressures operating at government and managerial levels. These exert their influence from the top down as well as the bottom up. Marcus Evans' paper memorably describes how uncontained NHS staff can feel, faced with the demands and distress of both patients and managers – a double load, if you like, of pressure and demand (Evans,

2015). The picture he paints is one in which managers, far from providing what clinical staff need in terms of support and containment for difficult, complex and highly responsible work, pass onto staff their own unprocessed anxieties about survival in a cut-throat environment.

The updated social defence paradigm goes some way towards explaining why staff may feel so ambivalent towards reflective practice. It reminds us that agendas in healthcare organisations are often multiple, and that the main task of the organisation is often not simply the care of patients. Managers, for example, have their own distinct worries and preoccupations, which a reflective practice group focusing purely on the concerns of ground-level staff may work against – or may be thought to work against, whatever the reality. The social defence paradigm, which sees social defences in healthcare organisations as emanating from a variety of sources, including both the clinical encounter and demands from government and society, offers the idea that the formulation of aims for any new reflective practice group should take account of the working environment of the staff who are attending. The focus will remain on their clinical practice, but it is helpful if the group is able to acknowledge competing pressures within their organisation, and even to find a way of addressing these and, thereby, ensuring a fuller acceptance of reflective practice in the organisation as a whole.

Empirical research does seem to suggest that the overall ethos of a service, and particularly the attitude of managers towards clinical supervision, is important in determining the influence of supervisory activity on clinical outcomes. The only randomised control study of the clinical impact of reflective supervision for nurses in a group setting produced disappointing results, but interviews with staff drew attention to the negative and distrustful attitude of managers towards the intervention (White & Winstanley, 2010). The authors concluded that this lack of support greatly limited the effectiveness of the supervision offered.

Research on clinical supervision suggests that the attitude of the organisation exerts an impact on supervisory outcomes via the extent to which it encourages attendance, and influences the manner in which the staff engages. It is a matter of both the quantity and quality of the provision of supervision. The overall level of participation by the staff is certainly significant: so, for example, in a study of 260 community mental health nurses, Edwards et al. (2005) found that supervision was rated as higher in quality if it lasted for over an hour and took place at least once a month. But it does not always seem to be a case of the more the better. As an example, Danish researchers Gonge and Buus

(2016, 2015) obtained mixed results in their investigations of the link between the level of participation in supervision by nursing staff and its perceived effectiveness. In one of their large studies, the amount of participation in supervision was associated with increased satisfaction with it; and in the other, it was not.

It seems likely that, as with therapy, the quality of the supervisory relationship is a key factor in determining success – and, of course, this applies to the relationship of the facilitator to a reflective practice group. So far the research points towards the value of staff being able to choose whether to attend reflective practice and who the facilitator is, with the additional suggestion that finding a protected space away from the usual work setting also makes a difference. A recent review of qualitative research into the effectiveness of Balint groups in medical training found that those who attended voluntarily were more likely to experience the group as helpful and effective, and those who felt coerced into going were less likely to have a positive experience (Monk, Hind & Crimlisk, 2018). And Edwards et al. (2005) found that the perceived quality of supervision was higher for those nurses who had chosen their supervisors, and where supervision took place away from their regular place of work.

The ideal situation is likely to be one in which reflective practice is integral to the service ethos, and staff are encouraged to attend, instead of being told to do so. The situation in which attendance of reflective practice is mandatory is to be avoided if possible. Overall the research evidence does seem to confirm the value of a focus within the Inter-subjective Model on communication with managers about the aims and objectives of reflective practice, as well as the practical issues involved in doing it successfully, with the purpose of promoting a supportive and informed attitude in the organisation.

Summary

- The stage of organisational contracting involves gathering information about the system-wide context for a request for a reflective practice group and keeping senior staff in the loop about developments, while preserving the boundaries of the group as a separate and safe place for the members.
- The practical aims at this stage are threefold: to open a channel of communication with managers to maximise their investment in reflective practice and their support for it; to educate managers about the value of reflective practice and its impact on clinical practice and staff well-being, thus developing reflective cultures in

healthcare; and to face up to the possibility that there is sometimes insufficient support for reflective practice to go ahead, and decide when this is the case.

- The concept of the social defence system is useful in understanding why reflective practice facilitators are sometimes met with such defensive reactions within services; it suggests the importance of developing reflective thinking at both the level of practitioner experience and the level of organisational structures and support, and explains why doing one without the other may be problematic.

- Facilitators should ensure they discuss any request for a reflective practice group with managers and senior staff in the service, letting them know about the plan and asking about desired outcomes from their perspective.

- Facilitators should ask for practical support to help ensure that the group runs smoothly before committing to facilitate the group, such as the use of a suitable room set apart from the usual working environment and arrangements that make it possible for staff to attend regularly.

- Facilitators often go ahead with a group without liaising with managers and senior staff, leaving the wider service context out of their thinking about the group's purpose. This can produce difficulties later on if the group has to operate without management buy-in and support, or members define their aims without reference to the overall service context.

- Groups can sometimes get taken over by concerns about what is going on in the organisation and the impact of this on staff, in which case, the task of the facilitator is to give some space to learning about contextual issues but to retain a focus on ground-level practice, making links between the two where relevant.

- Facilitators have a duty to take any serious concern about the safety of patients or staff to senior colleagues within the organisation, preferably with the cooperation, and always with the knowledge, of group members; the aim should be to lodge this with someone external to the group who is empowered to do something about it, and then to return to the reflective practice task.

- The significance of organisational support in influencing the effectiveness of reflective practice is indicated by a small but growing body of research. This suggests that the organisation has a key role to play in encouraging participation in reflective practice groups and communicating a positive attitude towards reflective practice, and that forcing staff to attend and turning reflective practice into a mandatory requirement is not helpful.

References

Armstrong, D. & Rustin, M. (Eds.) (2015) *Social defences against anxiety: explorations in a paradigm*. London: Karnac Books.

Edwards, D., Cooper, L., Burnard, P., Hannigan, B., Juggesur, T., Adams, J., Fothergill, A. & Coyle, D. (2005) Factors influencing the effectiveness of clinical supervision. *Journal of Psychiatric and Mental Health Nursing*, 12(4): 405–414.

Evans, M. (2015) 'I'm beyond caring': a response to the Francis Report. In Armstrong, D. & Rustin, M. (Eds.) *Social defences against anxiety: explorations in a paradigm*. London: Karnac Books.

Gonge, H. & Buus, N. (2016) Exploring organizational barriers to strengthening clinical supervision of psychiatric nursing staff: a longitudinal controlled intervention study. *Issues in Mental Health Nursing*, 37(5): 332–343.

Gonge, H. & Buus, N. (2015) Is it possible to strengthen psychiatric nursing staff's clinical supervision? RCT of a meta-supervision intervention. *Journal of Advanced Nursing*, 71(4): 909–921.

Hinshelwood, R.D. (1993) Locked in role: a psychotherapist within the social defence system of a prison. *Journal of Forensic Psychiatry*, 4: 427–440.

Jacques, E. (1955) Social systems as a defence against Persecutory and Depressive Anxiety. In Klein, M., Heimann, P. & Money-Kyrle, R.E. (Eds.) *New directions in psycho-analysis: the significance of infant conflict in the pattern of adult behaviour*. New York: Basic Books, Inc.

Kurtz, A. (2002) A psychoanalytic view of two forensic mental health services. *Criminal Behaviour and Mental Health*, 12: 68–80.

Menzies Lyth, I. (1960) A case study in the functioning of social systems as a defence against anxiety: a report on a study of the nursing service of a general hospital. *Human Relations*, 13(2): 95–121.

Monk, A., Hind, D. & Crimlisk, H. (2018) Balint groups in undergraduate medical education: a systematic review. *Psychoanalytic Psychotherapy*, 32(1): 61–86.

Rice, A.K. (1969) Individual, group and inter-group processes. *Human Relations*, 22: 565–584.

White, E. & Winstanley, J. (2010) A randomized controlled trial of clinical supervision: selected findings from a novel Australian attempt to establish the evidence base for causal relationships with quality of care and patient outcomes, as an informed contribution to nursing practice development. *Journal of Research in Nursing*, 15(2): 151–167.

3   Contracting and Review at the Group Level

What is Contracting and Review at the Group Level

The group contracting stage is when the group discusses its overall sense of purpose together with more specific aims for review, and the question of what structures and processes need to be put in place to support these. It is important that discussion of any contractual issues is informed by the group's understanding of its task; and, vice versa, that consideration of the group's purpose is informed by what is possible in practical terms within any given setting. This may seem an obvious point, but it is not uncommon for groups to separate the two, invoking a list of general ideas about good practice in running groups or defining the purpose of the group in a situation, which does not, and perhaps cannot, support this purpose.

Members' understanding of the task of the group is a crucial topic for discussion at the contracting stage. The most common reason given to me over the years for aversive experiences of reflective practice groups is the absence of a clearly defined group task, and the confusion and misunderstanding that result from this, particularly about whether to focus on personal material or not. Individual group members and other stakeholders will perhaps have different ideas about what is the purpose of the group, or what they want from it, and it is helpful to reach a broad agreement between members at this early stage, reminding them that the group's purpose can be reviewed going forward, and its focus may change over time.

Lawrence (1977), in his analysis of work groups, identified three different aspects to the primary task of any group: the normative aspect, which is the formally defined task or the official 'mission statement'; the existential aspect, which is the task that the group members think and believe they are engaged in; and the phenomenal aspect, which is the definition of the task that could be inferred by the behaviour of members of the group as seen and described by an outside observer. It is indeed the case that what people in a work group think they are doing may be different from what they are actually doing, and that both of these may be different from what stakeholders outside the group (such as senior staff who have commissioned the group) consider them to be doing. What is helpful at this stage is to clarify and explore varying ideas about what a reflective practice group is for, and build a reasonably simple, shared working definition of its purpose on which to base a contract and a system for review.

Apart from reflective practice there are three main types of group for healthcare staff, all of which have different but potentially overlapping aims with reflective practice. Sometimes a reflective practice group develops so that it is not clear what type of group it really is, and it is helpful to be able to track these changes.

We can start by reminding ourselves of a brief definition of reflective practice, which uses the resources of a group to develop thinking about problems and challenges in practice. Its methods may be diverse, but its aim is the development of practice. Next there is clinical supervision in a group setting, in which a small group of staff meets together with a supervisor to discuss their clinical work. This can, at the reflective end, be very similar to reflective practice (indeed, I would see reflective practice as close to what is referred to as reflective supervision, with the proviso that in reflective practice the supervisory resource is the group rather than an individual supervisor). There is a more didactic form of clinical supervision, in which the supervisor gives guidance and advice rather than fostering reflection, sometimes teaching the group a particular model or technique. At the management end, clinical supervision is about checking on the quality of practice and deciding what to do next. There is staff support, which is about improving the well-being of staff, often in the context of high rates of absence or sickness and low morale amongst staff. This tends to focus on what is going on in the organisation, on staff members' interactions with clients and colleagues and on how staff are feeling. And there is also organisational consultation, the aim of which is to improve some aspect of the way the organisation is functioning. This may be practical in its approach or may direct attention to a particular relationship between staff or the dynamics in a staff group or team.

This list is not by any means an exhaustive one. It is offered as a map to help reflective practice groups identify their purpose, and where this might overlap in some way with different but related group activities. All of these types of work groups are valuable in the right context. I think though that problems arise when one sort of group inadvertently develops into another; members can find themselves, for example, in a staff support group when they have agreed to reflective practice, or in a reflective practice group when what they really want is staff support. It is helpful for groups to know what they are doing and why, and to make conscious decisions about moves away from the agreed task. Flexibility may at times be just what is needed for a group to develop and grow; but persistently blurred boundaries around the nature of the task can be unhelpful, leading to the group feeling it has lost its way and to difficult and anxiety-provoking experiences for individual group members.

Once the purpose of the reflective practice group has been agreed, its aims can be derived from members' more specific ideas about how its progress on this task can be charted. So for example, if the purpose of a reflective practice group is to help a multidisciplinary team on a ward in thinking about the various in-patients who are staying there, the aims of the group might be to make sure that over a year all members get the chance to talk about their work with individual patients in some depth, in recognition of the fact that at the start of the group, members' confidence in sharing their practice with others varied enormously.

If the group knows what its main purpose is and has defined two to three aims for review, members can then discuss some of the more detailed aspects of how the group will run. I would suggest that this is done fairly briefly at first and then gone back to once or twice early on (say over the first three to five meetings). This is because group members often feel overwhelmed at the beginning and do not take things in, and relevant issues emerge through the real experience of the group and are hard to anticipate in the abstract. In the case of a group meeting monthly in an open-ended fashion, I would aim to have a contractual review at six-monthly points going forwards.

Safety, trust and confidentiality

In my view there are three main aspects to the development of safety and trust in a reflective practice group: the practical arrangements that are made to ensure privacy and confidentiality for group members and their clients, and to manage group boundaries and membership; the attitude of the facilitators and group members to one another, which should be positive and respectful and should also, over time, allow people to let down their guards and at times to be constructively critical; and last but not least, the attention to meaning-making activity within the group, so that reactions that may at first be troubling or puzzling are made sense of and brought back to the core aim of developing practice.

It is crucial that material is brought to reflective practice in such a way that the identities of clients are protected. When group members are working for the same healthcare organisation, as opposed to the same service, it is sometimes possible to lose sight of the importance of client confidentiality, and the facilitators need to help members keep this firmly in mind. Client material should always be brought in an anonymous form: names and identifying features should be changed or taken out, and sometimes, it may be necessary to fictionalise an aspect of the case to ensure real anonymity. For example, forensic patients often achieve a certain notoriety and details of cases are published in the media, so these individuals can only be properly disguised by taking out or changing characteristics or contextual aspects that are in the public domain. This should be carried out with some care, so that identities are protected without the issue the practitioner wants to talk about being too greatly altered. I have done this by changing the location of the service or the country of origin of the patient. Group members should let the group know when they have fictionalised an aspect of the case, but should not, of course, let them know what it is that they have changed.

In addition, some thought should be put into whether to protect the identities of staff in the practice situation which is shared in reflective practice. It may be important to do this if, for example, a member wants to talk about a difficult relationship with a colleague or problematic dynamics in a staff team. Ordinarily it is not necessary to protect the identities of colleagues spoken about in reflective practice in the same way as clients, as we are in public roles in our work in healthcare organisations. But it may be respectful, and indeed wise, to speak discretely. It is important to ensure that the reflective practice group does not descend into gossip.

As an overall rule of thumb, safety in a reflective practice group depends on the detail of what is spoken about within the group staying in the group. Members need to feel that the group is a protected space, in which they can share experiences and responses without them going elsewhere. The group may well give feedback to others in the service, but this should always be general and thematic rather than a leakage of what was actually said. Occasionally, however, there may be a need to take an issue outside the group. This can happen if the facilitator is seriously concerned about the practice of a group member, or something comes up which cannot be ignored, such as, for example, a safeguarding matter that is not being attended to. The facilitator may also be concerned about the attitude of a member towards the group, if for example, someone is persistently criticising the facilitator or their colleagues.

What should happen initially is for the group to discuss the matter directly, and usually, there will be no need for the facilitators to take the issue outside the group. But sometimes facilitators do feel they need to act outside the group, and when this happens, they should be open about the fact that they are doing this. These boundary matters are often tricky, and it is helpful for the facilitator to be able to discuss the issue with a colleague, and to check whether the concern is at a level which merits acting outside the group.

I have been involved several times in giving advice to facilitators running reflective practice groups for trainee clinical psychologists when they have developed concerns about an aspect of a trainee's practice. Through trial and error, we have developed a guideline, which is laid out in the following table. The facilitators should find a non-inflammatory way of letting the group know about their concern and their plan to meet with the individual outside the group to discuss it further. It is then possible to talk with the individual about the most helpful person to share the concern with, whether it be a manager or a clinical colleague. The key thing is to lodge the concern with someone who can do something about it, and then restore the previous boundaries of the group in a clear and calm way so the trust of the group is retained.

Although the practical arrangements which ensure confidentiality are very important, in my experience it is often the attitude of the group that matters most to members. Healthcare staff in large public organisations can feel demoralised and isolated, and it is helpful to create a positive and appreciative working culture in a reflective practice group, in which members are encouraged to notice and remark upon the often considerable skills and resources of their colleagues.

Table 3.1 Steps to follow when considering whether to take an issue of concern outside a reflective practice group

1	These boundary issues can be tricky: do some thinking in confidence with a supervisor or trusted colleague before you act
2	Let the group know, in a calm and measured way, of your concern and the plan to meet separately with the relevant group member to talk further about it
3	Explore the matter at this separate meeting and work together on a plan as to what should happen next
4	Action this plan, bearing in mind the aim of lodging concern with somebody who is in the position to take necessary action
5	Continue with the group, reinstating the boundaries that existed beforehand

I recently observed a reflective practice group on a training day, at which a senior nurse gained a great deal of support from the sympathetic responses of others to her feelings of being out of her depth in the face of the demands of patients. She had not talked about these feelings with colleagues before. The experience was a profound one: she had felt terribly alone in her work, and the realisation that others felt the same way had a dramatic and positive effect on her.

Safety and trust are promoted by a solid and shared sense of purpose in the group. This is, of course, something that is considered at the beginning, contractual stage of the group's life. But it is developed through the process of group meetings over time; it is dependent on the sense of containment offered by the dual ability of the group to, firstly, free itself to share material from practice and responses to the work and, secondly, to be thoughtful in developing a real understanding of the material shared. In other words, I believe that containment in reflective practice groups occurs by combining an opening-out process with a gathering-in one, bringing the group back to a focus on practice and grounding the work in a shared sense of purpose.

Space and time

The venue for reflective practice meetings must be a private space. It is no good, for example, trying to facilitate a reflective practice group in an open environment, which people are walking into and out of during the course of the meeting. It is best to have a private room, which can be booked regularly and in advance, and it is helpful if the room is at least at a certain distance from the pressures, and the potential intrusions, of a busy clinical environment. So for example, it can work well for nursing staff to go to a quiet room that is set apart from the ward, rather than to meet on an understaffed ward, facing interruptions because colleagues need help or advice.

The group will need to consider the time allocated for each reflective practice meeting. There are multiple pressures on healthcare staff today and so the question often arises as to how much time can be spared and whether this is enough. I tend to think of an hour as the minimum amount of time for a reflective practice group, and of an hour and a half as ideal. But it depends: if a group is meeting regularly, say weekly, it is possible to get into a rhythm and even to make a half-hour or forty-five-minute slot work. If a group is meeting less regularly, say monthly or bi-monthly, people will usually need more time to make the transition from busy work pressures to a reflective mode.

Next there is the question as to how far into the future to plan meetings. It can take a while for a group of staff to learn about reflective practice and what it can offer, and so it seems sensible to have a proper run of meetings before any review – say ten to twelve of them. I would think of a year of monthly meetings as a good initial plan for any staff team, with the aim of meeting for another year if all is going well.

It is also useful to plan a review and to at least consider the question of an ending, and interesting to observe that these are often not discussed. I have heard from quite a few colleagues who offer open-ended groups, sometimes in difficult circumstances, without an idea as to when the arrangement will be reviewed or will come to an end. An open-ended offer of this sort may well be just the thinking space which a group of healthcare staff needs. But if the group is finding it hard to make use of reflective practice, a review point or ending can provide a useful focus and help members face up to the challenge of the task. An open-ended offer may serve to communicate an unrealistic idea that the facilitators' resources are unlimited, and it may contribute to these resources – the facilitators' knowledge and expertise, their time and effort – being taken for granted and undervalued.

In addition, an open-ended offer can promote an unhealthy dependence on the facilitator, as if the group has to have them there to think in a certain way, rather than, over time, taking in what they have learnt from the group to influence their practice and the overall working culture of the service. The aim of reflective practice, after all, is to build up the thinking resources of a group of colleagues, which partly involves helping members to realise the resources they already possess. One could argue that this has been achieved when the facilitator becomes, at least in part, redundant. I took it as a sign of work well done when a group of colleagues who met for reflective practice with me as an external facilitator for a number of years decided to carry on meeting without me, taking it in turns to facilitate the group for each other.

Group boundaries and membership

Regular attendance by a stable group of staff is important in promoting the sense of a safe and cohesive group. This should be discussed at the start with the aim of promoting consistent attendance. It is also helpful for group members to let others know in advance wherever possible when they are unable to attend.

The problem of healthcare staff who have every good intention of attending reflective practice, but find themselves cancelling with increasing frequency because of the pressure of work, is a familiar one. If this happens it should not be avoided by the facilitator but sympathetically addressed. Clinical demands will always seem more pressing than reflective practice, certainly in the short-term, and, therefore, a reflective practice group will only work if there is recognition of the long-term value of a thinking space away from these demands. I do not think it is helpful to be rigid about attendance, or for attendance of a reflective practice group to be presented as mandatory. But it has a corrosive effect if people do not come and this goes unremarked upon. The facilitator can ask about reduced attendance, inquiring about outside pressures and also about members' feelings about the usefulness of the group. It may be that there is some dissatisfaction with how the group is running and that this needs to be looked at.

A reflective practice group is sometimes made up of colleagues who share a common task but do not work together on a daily basis. More often, it will consist of colleagues who have an ongoing working relationship, such as a group of ward staff or a healthcare team. Sometimes, people like the idea of being in a group with colleagues with whom they are familiar and by whom they feel supported. The advantage of working with a pre-existing group like this is that you can develop the reflective capacity of the overall team, so that colleagues are more able to draw on the resources of their colleagues outside as well as inside the group. But in reality the presence of close colleagues is often experienced as a problem, particularly if the relationship prevents or inhibits open talking about concerns at work. Unequal power relationships, such as those between managers and those who they manage, or trainees and tutors responsible for assessment, are the most common sources of tension. The inhibition is often a two-way one, although there is no doubt that it is more acute in staff who are in a less powerful position. Managers can feel anxious about letting more junior staff know about difficulties they are experiencing or areas of uncertainty; and more junior staff can feel unable to explore questions they have and expose messy, or at least unpolished, practice, in the presence of someone associated with a management or assessment function.

Therefore it is often helpful, indeed necessary, to keep reflective and governance activities separate, ensuring that staff and managers, or student practitioners and tutors, are not in the same group or involved in facilitating a group for one another. For example, on the clinical psychology training course where I work, I do not facilitate reflective practice for trainees who I manage. I share line management duties with a colleague, so when I take on a new group for reflective practice, I make sure that the trainees I manage are in the other group. According to the same principle, when my academic colleagues facilitate reflective practice groups they organise the allocation of marking so they are not responsible for assessing the work of trainees in their group.

There is, however, sometimes a case for having a mixture of staff at different levels of a hierarchy in the same group, or at least for considering this as a possibility. The reason for this is that facilitation of a mixed group is more likely to produce change at the cultural or service level. It can be effective in creating a more open-minded, tolerant and arguably, more robust, working environment than existed before, rather than going along with a split whereby reflective practice is developed in isolation and staff feel increasingly at odds with the overall working environment. The facilitation of mixed groups can prove a useful intervention in a circular process: if managers develop a reflective ethos alongside their staff, the latter will feel more comfortable talking openly about clinical issues with them. The facilitation of segmented groups risks collusion with the idea that honesty about the realities of clinical practice is not compatible with a management or assessment perspective, when in my view, what we are working towards is a healthcare system in which reflective practice is integral to the way a clinical service operates and develops over time. The two perspectives are, of course, different, and bringing them together is a complicated and challenging matter. But they are not – and should not be – necessarily distinct.

Group membership and potential boundary problems are best discussed at the outset, when the possibility of a group is first mooted. The group needs to feel safe enough to start to share experiences from practice openly and, if having staff at different levels of the organisational hierarchy will make this difficult, they should be put into separate groups at this point. One possibility is to begin with groups in which senior staff meet separately from ground-level practitioners, and create mixed groups at a later stage, when practitioners feel comfortable with a reflexive approach and confident that it is supported by those at all levels of the organisation. If managers and ground-level staff are together in a reflective practice group, a discussion should take place about how to protect a thinking space for everyone. A first step is the acknowledgement of the worry practitioners may have about provoking a managerial, top-down response if they talk about a clinical worry or concern, and that managers may have about opening up and appearing not to be in control. A reflective space, in which the roles and the familiar activities associated with these roles are held in suspension, at least for a period, must be protected by the group. The implications of the group's reflections on practice can be considered at the Turning Out stage, but should be held in abeyance until then.

The question of whether to have an external or an internal facilitator

Some services have the funding available to commission an external facilitator for a reflective practice group; but in many cases, a facilitator needs to be found within the organisation. It is usually assumed that it is better to have an external facilitator. Overall this is probably the case, since when someone comes in from outside, they have a fresh perspective on the work of the service, and it is easier for the group to see reflective practice as separate from ongoing work pressures. However, the internal facilitator has a definite advantage in that they will have built up an understanding of the needs of the service, and will be known to group members and hopefully trusted by them. The main difficulty facing the internal facilitator is keeping in the role when they have an existing working relationship with group members, and are themselves involved in many of the activities discussed by the group. It is all too easy for the internal facilitator to get drawn into discussions and not to pay attention to how the group is functioning in relation to its task. For this reason, if a facilitator needs to be found within the organisation, it is best if they are somewhat removed from the day-to-day work of group members. I know of a service in which this is achieved by a small network of staff internal to the organisation who facilitate groups in teams other than their own. There are about ten of them, and they facilitate reflective practice groups in each other's teams. This ensures a useful degree of externality in facilitation across all the groups, but no one needs to be paid to come in from outside.

Record keeping

The purpose of a written record is to remind members of what was discussed in previous sessions, particularly before reviews or the provision of feedback to managers. Often, the facilitator of a reflective practice group will keep the written record for the group, but it promotes ownership of the group by its members if the responsibility for writing a brief record of its activities is rotated amongst members. It should be decided when the record will be destroyed. I would suggest that records are not kept for longer than one year after meetings have taken place.

Record keeping can be a useful means of communication for a large staff group, in which colleagues are able to attend some but not all reflective practice sessions. In these circumstances, the written record is shared by everyone and becomes a way of joining with the group experience when actual attendance is not possible. These records tend to be fuller and more detailed than for groups where all are present, and therefore, it is important that the record is only shared within the membership and is destroyed after an agreed period of time.

Critical issues from practice

All too often, contracting at the group level takes place without any reference to the organisational context, as if the group existed in isolation from the service as a whole. Discussion about arrangements for the group should at least makes reference to service aims and the purpose of reflective practice from the point of view of senior staff. This does not mean that the aims of the group at the organisational and the group level must be the same, only that both need to be borne in mind at the contractual stage. This is especially useful in preparing the group to provide feedback to managers, which involves framing the activities of the group in relation to a management agenda – or at least trying to do so. The task of the facilitator here is to achieve some sort of integration between these two areas of activity, and in so doing, to work towards creating a supportive overall context for reflective practice and reducing organisational ambivalence.

Another common problem that occurs at the group contracting stage is that discussion takes place rather hastily at the beginning, and is not informed by actual experiences of working in the group. It is as if this stage is something to get through before making a real start on things. This can result in rather dry, abstract contracting, which does not take account of the most useful areas for any particular group and is hard to operationalise. As an example, on the Leicester clinical psychology training course, we did not anticipate that the way in which trainees within the wider cohort talk about what is going on in their respective reflective practice groups, each of which is made up of half of the year group, would be an especially significant issue. At the contracting stage, we always considered the importance of protecting the identity of clients and group members, ensuring that responses of individuals were not discussed outside. However, it turned out that the groups were often very interested in what went on in the other group, and it was unrealistic to expect trainees not to have comparative discussions. We revised our arrangement, suggesting that trainees

Table 3.2 Group contracting issues and summary of advice

Contractual issue	Summary of advice	Points for consideration
Confidentiality for clients and discretion for professional colleagues	Material identifying clients should be taken out or changed; where possible, identities of staff should be protected and discretion about professional matters encouraged	Is material being spoken about in front of people outside the clinical service, in which case, the confidentiality of patients should be ensured? Are issues regarding colleagues processed in a respectful and productive way?
Confidentiality for group members	The detail of what is discussed in the group should be kept in the group; communication outside the group, for e.g. when feeding back to managers, should be thematic and general	Group members can find it hard to talk about safety within the group, so check on this at review points
Management of boundaries: when a safeguarding or performance issue needs to be raised outside the group	Talk this through with a supervisor or trusted colleague before acting; let the group know what is happening, discuss the issue separately with the group member concerned, lodge the issue with the relevant colleague and reinstate the group's boundaries as before	Is the issue sufficiently concerning to merit external consideration?
Stability of membership	Attendance should be voluntary with an expectation of regular and consistent attendance	The more stable the membership the better, but if some staff cannot attend every time, specify minimum expectation of attendance
Group membership	It is often best to separate managers and ground-level staff into different groups, although if they feel safe together reflective practice can then develop at the service level	Things can change over time and it is a sign of progress at the service level if managers and staff feel comfortable working together in a group when they did not previously

Contractual issue	Summary of advice	Points for consideration
Length of each group session	1 hour minimum, 1.5 hours ideal (less than this can work if the group meets more often than monthly)	Is the time allocated long enough? If not, consider meeting more frequently or less often and for longer
Length of the group overall	Reviews should be at least six-monthly; arrange to meet initially for a year with a plan for either an open-ended group afterwards or a group for a finite period of two to three years	Is it best to set up an open-ended group or a time-limited one? Don't jump into offering an open-ended group too soon, but base your decision on the resources available and the motivation of staff
Where will the group meet?	Regular use of a room that is set apart from a busy clinical environment is a basic requirement; a quiet, comfortable and spacious room is ideal	Do consider rearranging the furniture so group members are as comfortable as possible
External/internal facilitation	External facilitation is usually best, but if this is not possible, the facilitator should be removed from the day-to-day work of group members (for e.g. facilitators swapping to run groups across services); and/or have access to supervision to help them keep in role	Has the facilitator, external or internal, got the support they need? An external facilitator will need good links with the service and the support of managers; an internal facilitator needs access to supervision to help them keep in role
Written record	It is best for the responsibility for a written record to be rotated amongst members to describe discussions thematically rather than in detail and to be kept for a year and then destroyed	What is the purpose of any written record? If it is to inform reviews and feedback to managers, it does not need to be kept beyond a year; remind members to destroy notes if they have been circulated during the year

could talk in general terms about what was going on in their respective groups, but should not go into detail in relation to clients, clinical colleagues or individual group members.

A related difficulty is contractual discussion which is not properly informed by the sense of the group's overall purpose. It is not unusual to hear about a reflective practice group that has moved into consideration of details, such as how to ensure a due degree of privacy and safety, where and how often to meet, who will come and so on, without reference to a shared understanding of the main task of the group. Quite often guidelines are borrowed from experiences of staff support or group therapy, rather than reflective practice in a healthcare context. As an example, staff will talk about the need for absolute confidentiality. Group therapy, as opposed to reflective practice, does require careful protection of the confidentiality of all members, and for this reason, it is important that conversations about the group simply do not take place outside. By contrast, reflective practice for a group of colleagues may have an explicit and legitimate influence on discussions and actions that take place in the service at other times. Hopefully this influence will be a positive one, as long as members are able to preserve a space for thinking in the group without immediate recourse to action and instruction, and can maintain the privacy of individual colleagues in relation to the details of their practice and their responses to the practice of others.

Reflection practice groups can also set themselves up as one thing but turn into something else, as in the case of a group with the intention of focussing on issues from clinical practice, which finds itself functioning as a staff support or therapy group. It is quite normal for a group to shift between modes in this way for a limited period of time, either within the space of a single reflective practice session or for a few sessions. Sometimes this needs to happen in the name of exploration: after all, how does one know in advance whether a response is a personal matter or an important clue about what is going on in the clinical situation? Sometimes groups need to try something to find out. The problem arises when the transition remains unnoticed and becomes permanent or semi-permanent.

In their 1960s paper on the use of small training groups for general practitioners, Gosling and Turquet (1967) describe the need for facilitators to tolerate a certain amount of healthy regression in these work groups, in the same way as clinically sensitive doctors learn to accommodate healthy regression in their patients. It is well worth being reminded of this at a time when tolerance of ordinary regression in patients and staff in the NHS is particularly low, demanding that staff work without space for thought or recovery, and that patients fit in with what is seen as the most cost-effective treatment on offer and – to put it bluntly – get better fast or else. Healthy regression is all about going backwards in developmental terms in order to then go forwards; it is often a helpful process, representing a return to the point when things went wrong. Regression is unhealthy when it gets stuck or has an addictive quality to it, but it has an important part to play in creating the conditions for deep learning. In the reflective practice context, it may be that a group needs to move through a rather anxious or collapsed period, behaving passively and requiring instruction from the facilitator, for example, or appearing immobilised by anxiety and unable to think. It may feel as if the group is going off course. If this is so, a review provides an opportunity to restore the group's original sense of purpose. But it may well be that the shift is best viewed as part of the group's journey and a means to the end originally agreed by the group. Members may well need to explore an area of real anxiety or uncertainty before they can move forward in a more purposeful fashion. If this is what is happening, a statement from the facilitator about the value of such explorative phases will be very containing and will reconnect the group to its overall sense of its task.

Illustration: a training group is thrown by normal beginner anxiety, showing the value of revisiting contractual discussions and grounding them in specifics

This example comes from a two-day training course on how to run reflective practice groups, which I delivered to twenty or so multi-disciplinary colleagues from a healthcare trust in a rural part of the country. I have chosen it because those who attended this particular course focused their discussions on contracting processes and on the difficulty of seeing contractual discussions through satisfactorily at the start of a group, when both facilitators and members are finding their feet.

On the afternoon of the first day, I asked the participants to practise working through the stages of the Intersubjective Model, as I usually do. I offered the choice of working as one large group or breaking into two smaller groups, and they chose to stay as a single group. In retrospect this was a mistake on my part, as twenty is well over the optimum number for a reflective practice group and is likely to feel too exposing, particularly for participants who do not know each other and are only meeting in the context of a one-off course. Two people volunteered to act as a facilitating pair, and three others volunteered to be observers, sitting on the outside of the circle and watching how the group approached the task it had been given.

The reflective practice group started, and members were immediately struck by how different it felt actually being in a group, rather than talking about reflective practice groups in the abstract. The facilitators' first job was to discuss some form of minimal contract for this one-off group. This should have involved reminding one another of the purpose of the exercise and talking about what would be necessary to support this. But this turned out to be not at all straightforward: people spoke about being anxious and not knowing where to start. A few members then said they felt very unsure of what the task was, and there was even a slightly accusatory tone to these comments, as if the exercise had not been set up properly. The facilitators did their best, suggesting that clients' material should be anonymised and that we would only refer outside the group to what was discussed in thematic and non-specific terms. But overall, there was a sense that contracting was rushed and not based on the group's understanding of its task – indeed, that it had taken place in the absence of such understanding.

Next day I decided to keep things as simple as possible, and to show those on the course that contracting is something that is easiest to think about when it is grounded in a sense of the task and linked to specific experiences, either those which are anticipated, or those which have happened and can be used to adjust the way the group approaches its work. I decided to demonstrate facilitation of the Generation stage of the Intersubjective Model, helping one of the participants to share material which would lend itself to reflective practice, after carrying out some contractual discussion about how best to set up the demonstration.

The woman who had volunteered to share a dilemma from practice and I sat in front of the group, but we turned our chairs so we were looking at each other and could, as far as possible, forget about our audience. I started by reminding both of us of what we were doing, which was helping her to share her experience as fully as possible, and in a way which lent itself to colleagues' reflection on her practice. I asked how she was feeling about doing this and she said she felt okay; her only concern was that the details of what she was going to talk about should stay in the room. She said this a couple of times, and we agreed that this was a clear part of our agreement in doing the exercise. She was pretty sure that those listening would not know the people and places she was going to talk about, or feel compromised by the material she was planning to share, and I suggested that if this turned out not to be the case, individuals should bring this up and we should think about it together at the end of the afternoon. Before she started to speak, I asked what she wanted to gain from the reflections of her colleagues, and she was able to give some useful guidance. I had felt anxious at the start of the demonstration, but after this initial discussion, it felt as if we were walking on solid ground together and would be able to consider issues that might come up along the way.

Techniques

The key technical question at the group contracting stage is the extent to which to adopt a formal approach, going through arrangements systematically and in one go, or a fluid one, in which issues regarding structure and process are discussed in a more organic way as they come up. The former is more likely to cover all the important areas but may not include the detail relevant to the actual concerns and anxieties of the group; the latter can emerge more closely from the group's experiences, but risks, particularly if nothing is written down, something being missed or a misunderstanding occurring about what has been agreed.

A hybrid approach often works best. I would recommend going through contractual issues at the start and returning to them over the first few meetings in the light of experiences of working in the group, giving five minutes or so at the end to reviewing the meeting and discussing any practical issue that has come up. This should ensure that all the relevant areas are covered. I would also suggest producing a written document, which summarises the agreement made by the group over the course of its first few meetings. It promotes ownership of the contract by the group if it can be drafted and circulated for comments by a willing group member, rather than this task falling automatically to the facilitator.

Key influences

Wilfred Bion's work on group dynamics, and particularly his concept of a group mentality driven by what he described as a basic assumption (BA), has influenced my approach to contracting (Bion, 1961). BA group mentality is when an underlying assumption exerts a powerful and often unconscious influence on a group, interfering with the group's ability to get on with its working task. A basic assumption is a type of group fantasy, often unconscious. An individual's fantasy can be opened up and explored as an aspect of the internal world of a single human being; but it is more difficult to get at a group's fantasy, and in the main, this is done by making inferences on the basis of the way a group behaves. The facilitator can get a sense of its shape and character by asking themselves what is implied by behaviour, which often runs counter to the conscious, surface-level activity of the group in question.

The purpose of contracting – to develop an agreement about the best processes and practical arrangements to support the work of the group – is an important one; and yet in my experience, this activity is often carried out in a cursory way, or dealt with in a general and tokenistic manner. There is often a rather narrow focus on client confidentiality, an issue with which clinicians are familiar. Alternatively, if potential difficulties are brought to the group's attention, they tend to create a great deal of anxiety and are difficult to move beyond. What is going on in the case of what I would define as tokenistic or over-anxious contracting, and how might this inform thinking about how to approach this stage more productively?

The basic assumption of the group in these cases seems to be that situations that would be addressed by a proper contract, such as how to promote safety and trust in the group and how to manage difficulties, will never really come up but are put into the realm of unreality. What then takes place is a tick box exercise, in which contractual discussions take place, but they are rather thin and hard to relate to anything that might actually happen. On the other hand, if potential problems are brought to the group's attention and made to feel like real possibilities, they are overwhelming. The other aspect of this basic assumption seems to be the idea that if a problem were to occur, the group would not be able to cope.

This is not surprising given how anxious facilitators and group members usually feel at the start of a reflective practice group. In the beginning, the group will not yet have developed a solid sense of its purpose and mode of operation, and both facilitators and members will find it difficult to think in a sensible way about potential difficulties and how to address them. Contracting is too important to deal with only at the beginning of the life of a group. It seems sensible to start this stage when the group first meets, but then to continue with it over the first few meetings and revisit it at review points. In this way, a contractual discussion that takes place in the grip of an anxious stab at getting things right when the group first meets is avoided; and instead, the group is supported in thinking about its arrangements in the light of lived experience of its activities and interactions.

Mark Loveder (2017) did an in-depth study of the experiences of trainee clinical psychologists in a monthly reflective practice group, which contributed to my view that contracting is best thought of as a process rather than a one-off activity. I acted as the academic supervisor for his study, and the group was facilitated by two clinical colleagues. Loveder carried out a Grounded Theory analysis of transcripts from tapes of six reflective practice group sessions, focusing on those aspects of the process which were likely to influence clinical outcomes, such as discussion of feelings about clients or changes in the way in which clients' difficulties were conceptualised. He followed this first analytic stage up with interviews of individual members of the group, in which he tested out his emerging theory of the way in which reflective practice influenced the clinical situation.

The core category which Loveder developed was called 'Deepening Understanding in the Context of Building Trust'. It described the way in which trust in the group determined the extent to which members felt able to talk openly about struggles in their practice, and thereby to use the group as a way of deepening their understanding of clients and their interactions with them. Development of understanding was seen as the main way in which reflective practice in a group setting impacted on clinical outcomes. The feeling of trust and safety in the group was mediated by careful and ongoing observation of the way in which people reacted to honest sharing, either of struggles from clinical practice or of ideas and opinions about the clinical work of others.

Loveder's study reinforces the value of contracting at the group level as a process rather than a one-off activity, and suggests that anxiety about exposure should be a particular focus. It underscores the primary importance of an atmosphere of trust to the creative work of a reflective practice group, and of the ongoing way in which this is calibrated by members during the life of the group. Contracting is not something that is done and dusted at the beginning of a group, but is instead a continual process, particularly if it takes account not only of the explicit arrangements made by the group but of what is implicitly observed by group members over time and often goes unremarked upon. It is useful to make a distinction between the explicit and the implicit contract, the former consisting of what is written down by the group and the latter of observations of what really happens. Ideally, the two should be brought together as part of the review process.

Summary

- The stage of Contracting and Review at the Group Level is when the group discusses what arrangements it requires to support its work; it should be preceded by consideration of the overall purpose of the group, including the development of a shared understanding by stakeholders as to the definition of the reflective practice task.

- It is not uncommon for the boundaries between the activities of a reflective practice group and different types of related group, such as staff support, to become blurred; this can be useful for exploratory purposes but problems arise when the change is not acknowledged or a focus on reflective practice is not regained.
- Initial discussion of contractual issues can be unhelpfully brief and abstract or, alternatively, staff may become overwhelmed by the prospect of things going wrong and find it difficult to move on; for this reason, consideration of arrangements should be followed up by further discussion, so these can be reviewed in the light of experiences of work in the group.
- A key task of the facilitator during contracting is to help staff address real issues that may come up in a reflective practice group without getting taken over by anxiety.
- Safety and trust are dependent on arrangements that ensure confidentiality for clients and group members, and discretion when it comes to sharing information about colleagues; they also rely on a positive and respectful attitude of group members to the contributions of others, and the ability to follow up on the discussion of feelings and responses with thinking about what they mean in relation to practice, returning to a shared sense of the group's purpose.
- If the facilitator thinks that a concern might need to be taken outside the group, they should first sound things out with a supervisor or trusted colleague to help make up their mind; if they do decide to follow things up externally, they should do this in a clear and calm way, letting the group know of their plan, meeting with the group member concerned and communicating with those who have responsibility and power to act, with the aim of restoring group boundaries as quickly as possible.
- Group meetings should take place in a private setting, ideally set apart from busy clinical environments and possible interruptions, and should take place regularly, for example at fortnightly or monthly intervals for a minimum of an hour.
- Reviews should take place every six months at least and a decision should be made as to whether the group is finite or open-ended; finite groups should last for a minimum of a year but two to three years is better, and an open-ended group should only be offered if the group is making good use of reflective practice.

- Usually, the staff at different hierarchical levels in the organisation should be in separate groups to keep reflective and governance activities distinct; however, mixed groups provide an opportunity to develop reflective practice at the service level and may be considered if the staff feel safe enough.
- External facilitation usually requires additional resources but provides a fresh perspective and creates the sense of reflective practice as a valued and distinct activity; internal facilitation can feel more comfortable for the staff and is less expensive, but an internal facilitator should always have access to supervision to help maintain their role.
- A record of sessions can be useful when preparing for reviews, providing feedback to managers and keeping a large staff group connected to reflective practice when people are not able to attend every time; it is best if notes are not kept for more than a year, are thematic and general, conveying a sense of topics discussed rather than the details of practice, and if responsibility for note-taking is shared amongst members.
- Contracting can be done as a one-off activity with the production of a written contract, or in a more fluid way; a hybrid approach is recommended in which discussions over initial meetings are summarised in a document, ensuring that everything is covered and understanding is shared amongst group members.
- The stage of Contracting and Review at the Group Level is best thought of as an ongoing process, in which an initial agreement can be revised at reviews in the light of experience.

References

Bion, W. (1961) *Experiences in groups.* London: Tavistock Publications Ltd.

Gosling, R. & Turquet, P.M. (1967) The training of general practitioners. In Gosling, R., Miller, D.H., Woodhouse, D. & Turquet, P.M. *The use of small groups in training.* Hertfordshire: Codicote Press.

Lawrence, G. (1977) Management development . . . some ideals, images and realities. In Coleman, A.D. and Geller, M.H. (Eds) *Group relations reader 2.* Washington, DC: A.K. Rice Institute Series.

Loveder, M. (2017) *Does reflective practice impact upon clinical outcomes and if so, how? A grounded theory study of how trainee clinical psychologists experience the effect of a reflective practice group on their clinical work.* Unpublished Dissertation; University of Leicester.

4 Turning In

What is Turning In?

The Turning In stage involves the transition of group members from the concerns and pressures of day-to-day work in healthcare to a reflective, perspective-taking mode. The shift is from external movement and action to a comparatively still and thoughtful way of being. Healthcare staff attending reflective practice groups often work in challenging environments in which they are dealing with high levels of pain and distress, whether it be physical or mental in nature, and, sometimes, with aggression and violence as well. In most parts of the world, healthcare services are stretched, sometimes severely so. In the National Health Service in the United Kingdom, for example, practitioners have had to deal in recent years with drastic cuts to services and staffing in the face of increasing demand. Staff often feel demoralised and overwhelmed, and very much in need of offloading and support. This is entirely understandable, and facilitators will feel sympathetic and concerned when such feelings are expressed. However, there is a judgement call to be made about the point at which to turn to the task at hand: about how to get the balance right for the group, allowing enough time to absorb valuable contextual information and provide necessary support, without allowing the purpose of sharing and thinking together about clinical practice to be lost. If those attending remain in a reactive mode for too long and do not make the transition to a different form of thinking and feeling, they will be doing without the nourishment of the group's reflective resources at a time when they are probably in particular need of it. In the end, they are likely to feel stuck and dissatisfied.

Some facilitators enable the transition to a reflective mode in an active and explicit way, and some take a quieter and less obvious approach. But what is important is to be aware of the fact that members of the group will need to make this shift in one way or another. The transition can also sometimes feel unexpectedly difficult, and it is helpful not to be too thrown by this.

Without direct experience of a reflective practice group, it would be possible to imagine that members would enter – or even fall into – a reflective space with ease and a sense of relief. After all, reflective practice is intended as a space away from the active and challenging demands of clinical work. Surely then it would feel a little like a holiday or a break? Experience, however, teaches us otherwise. Time and again, when I have started to run a reflective practice group, even for experienced staff who expect to move easily into a reflective mode, members are struck by how hard it feels to start to engage with practice in front of colleagues in an open and reflective way.

What is this difficulty about? There is no doubt that it is partly to do with anxiety about sharing experiences from practice in unfamiliar ways in front of colleagues. In comparison with the setting for a reflective practice group, the external work environment is usually highly structured, and people often have quite distinct roles and functions within it. It can feel scary to enter an open space in which people can get to know each other in the work they do in a different, and hopefully a more three-dimensional, way. These anxieties tend to diminish if the group is felt to be a safe and supportive one, allowing room for curiosity and exploration, while retaining a focus on clinical practice and balancing a positive appreciation of members' contributions with criticism when it is genuinely constructive. These fears do not entirely disappear, however, and can reemerge from time to time, particularly at the start of group meetings. Indeed, I have come to see them as part of the creative process of reflective practice.

There are important biological and neurophysiological aspects to this shift as well. Staff coming into a reflective practice group from responsible and challenging clinical jobs are often stressed, and it can take a while for them to feel physically settled and calm. They will sometimes comment on how agitated they feel, and on how they notice this more when they remove themselves from a busy environment. We know that under stress, the emotional brain becomes activated and initiates the body's response to a threat, releasing cortisol and adrenaline and sending impulses via the sympathetic nervous system to increase our blood pressure and heart rate, and to pass oxygen and energy to our muscles (Freeman & Freeman, 2012). The body goes into a fight or flight mode, and we feel nervous and agitated. It can be difficult to step down from this charged, action-oriented state. It has a compelling, even an addictive, aspect to it, as well as being demanding and exhausting.

Some of the exciting new discoveries from neuroscience suggest why it is important, and also difficult, for healthcare staff to make the transition from a stressed, emotionally charged state to a more reflective and analytical one. Brain imaging techniques show heightened activation in the emotional or limbic brain system in response to stress or trauma, just as we would expect (van Der Kolk, 2014). They also show the extent of the deactivation of both the prefrontal cortex and the left brain, which are responsible for the executive functions of the mind and for language and analytic thought. When we are stressed and aroused, our body moves into a defensive, active mode, and as a consequence, it becomes difficult to think and plan properly.

However, what is less well-known is the extent to which when stressed it becomes difficult to empathise and relate to others. The prefrontal cortex, deactivated at times of heightened stress, is not only responsible for planning and analytic thought; it is also the seat of empathy, linguistic communication and processing of more complex and ambiguous information relating to relationships. We know from research into therapeutic outcomes how important it is for clients to experience empathy and a positive but realistic relationship with their therapist, a connection which can survive difficulties and enable learning from them (Norcross, 2011). It seems that providing staff in pressured clinical environments with protected space to think is not just important for their own well-being. Without opportunities to consider matters in a calm, safe environment, access to the parts of the mind and body which allow relational thinking and feeling to take place is likely to be greatly reduced, and relationships with clients will suffer accordingly.

Research on traumatic stress indicates that the stressed, active mode can become habitual and even addictive (van der Kolk, 2014). When a threat in the environment is removed in the ordinary scheme of things, the body returns from a heightened state of readiness for action to normal. However, when stress is acute and/or when it persists, the body's stress response reduces but does not disappear, as if the emotional brain is warning of the need to remain on guard. We also know that the body produces its own powerful analgesics; these are released in highly stressful situations, which offers an explanation at the biological level of why those who are stressed and suffering might sometimes appear to seek out further stress, or to find it difficult to walk away from extreme situations (Solomon, 1989; van der Kolk, 1989).

All of this means that facilitators often describe finding it surprisingly difficult to shift a group from an outward-facing, busy mode to a reflective one. They can feel as if they have to be quite firm in enabling this move, pushing members to do something they feel, hopefully only temporarily, unwilling to do. I have come to understand this as an aspect of this transitional stage: of the periodic reemergence of anxiety about entering an unfamiliar and potentially exposing space with work colleagues, and of the habitual quality of the body's response to stress, particularly in more highly charged healthcare environments. The facilitator can help the group make this shift if they remain unfazed by what is likely to be a passing reluctance to shift into a reflexive mode, confident that the group will gain from making the transition to thinking in a different way about their work.

Critical issues from practice

It can happen that staff attending a reflective practice group do not manage to leave external pressures and concerns behind, and remain in a preoccupied state for the duration of the meeting. The context for this is often one in which the outside events that are reported by staff, often organisational matters, have a vivid or an urgent quality to them. For example, news may be shared to which colleagues inevitably have strong reactions, such as information about job losses and service closures. Usually the facilitator will feel very sympathetic towards staff. At any rate, the issue seems too important to simply put to one side. On the other hand, the facilitator may also have doubts about the value of letting the discussion of the matter take over the group, and may even have a question about what is being avoided by a focus on this type of external matter. They may also be anxious about cutting across such discussions amongst staff who seem vulnerable and overwhelmed, feeling that it would be insensitive to do so. This worry is likely to be particularly acute if the facilitator works in the same team or service, rather than coming in from outside, and is, therefore, caught up in whatever is being spoken about.

It is usually best to move group members away from general organisational matters to hear about a specific aspect of their working life and practice, the Generation stage, but only after giving some time to discussion of the wider issue. I have sometimes given a full group meeting to the discussion of general service issues in order to regain a focus on reflective practice at the next meeting. These matters, after all, provide the context for ground-level work in healthcare, and an appreciation of the characteristics of the wider environment may well enrich the quality of the group's reflections on an individual's experience from practice. But the facilitator should be aware of the downside of doing too much of this. I have spoken quite a few times to facilitators who feel their group has become stuck in a rather passive, complaining mode. It could be that a preoccupation with problems 'out there' has become a way of avoiding looking at the practice of individuals and bumping up against the differences in style or opinion of people in the group. Or it may be that a staff group is just very pressured and used to functioning on adrenaline, and they are in the grip of a habit of coping at work that is hard to shift.

An alternative problem is when the transition to a reflective mode appears to be smooth and it seems as if the group is getting on with the work, but external stresses continue to exert an influence in an unspoken way and compromise the group's capacity for depth and openness in their thinking. The facilitator tends to learn about this difficulty slowly, through a gradual but definite sense of an 'as if' quality to discussions in the group. Group members are doing what they should be doing but in a constrained or somewhat superficial way, and the group is not developing over time as it could do. The facilitator intuits that something is going on of which they are unaware, either within the group itself or in the external environment, but does not know how to address this because they have very little information to go on. My approach to these situations is generally to try to say something to open up discussion, offering an observation about what is appearing difficult and asking what might be done to shift things or make things easier. Sometimes this makes it possible for a problem or pressure to be named and, sometimes, it does not. But it is worthwhile for the facilitator to let group members know that they are available for consideration of the impact of general external difficulties, in case there comes a time when this can make a positive difference.

Illustration: a co-facilitator and I initially find it hard to help a well-established group make the transition to reflective practice, but manage to get there in the end

A colleague Miranda and I had been facilitating a reflective practice group for six trainee clinical psychologists for the past two years, and met recently with them for the first meeting of their third and final year of training after a long summer break. This is a group who took naturally to reflective practice from the start: they were quite open with one another about feelings and concerns relating to their clinical work, and also appeared comfortable enough to express a variety of views and reactions, and to show appreciation of the unique contribution each member makes to the seminar.

At the start Miranda and I talked about how long it had been since we last met. One member said it felt amazing and also unreal to think they were now in their final year of training. Miranda and I asked them about this. At this point I imagined that we would spend ten minutes or so talking about their experiences of starting the third year, before moving on to hear about an issue from the clinical placements they had recently finished.

The trainees recalled their impressions from when they started the course of the trainees in the third and final year. The third years had seemed impressive, even intimidating, and had appeared to be almost in a different world from them as first-years and newbies. The third years seemed to know what they were doing and to present themselves in a highly professional manner; whereas they, as first years, felt anxious and uncertain, and far from being the accomplished professionals that they saw in the third years. It was strange to think that they might now strike the incoming first years in the same way. They did not feel on the inside like they thought they might look from the outside, especially to the new trainees.

This was an animated discussion, which led to some interesting thoughts, such as the psychological purpose of fixing on an individual or a group a bit further along any developmental path or trajectory, feeling inspired by and emulating them, as well as sometimes comparing oneself negatively and feeling demoralised. After about twenty minutes (more time than we would usually give to a check-in), I asked how people thought we should use the time and whether anyone had something they wanted to think about with the group. Someone responded by saying they felt distant from clinical placements, which had finished some time ago. Discussion continued in a rather abstract way about how the group felt about being in the final year of training and the prospect of being fully qualified in a year's time.

In the coffee break, Miranda and I talked about the difficulty of getting someone to bring an experience in lived detail to the group; the trainees were between clinical placements, but when this had happened previously they had wanted to return to think together about past cases. We noticed the discussion was beginning to feel a bit thin and empty, and we thought about how different it felt when we had some material from practice to work with. We agreed to go with the group's focus on their new identity as third years, to try to prompt some thinking about what this might mean in relation to the clients they would meet on their new placements the following week, and to ensure a return to generating material from their clinical experience at the next meeting.

After the break, Miranda said that, generally, it was useful to keep a focus on an experience from practice, but today it had been helpful to think about what it meant to go into the third year. One group member then responded by saying it felt as if the group did not have an anchor. I asked what thoughts people had about their identity as third years and meeting new clients on placement next week. There was more discussion, of a different, more engaged sort from the beginning, about how disconnected they felt from the placements they had finished a few weeks ago. There was then a conversation about how anxious they had been at the beginning of training about going into clinical sessions with clients. They had reassured each other that they could do it, and they had felt the need to arm themselves with plenty of materials so they could fill the time. They no longer felt the need to do this. They thought they now had greater inner resources as practitioners, and were more able to deal with the individual and the unexpected. This was a big change, and they were now more ready to engage at a human level with clients. The group seemed to be looking forwards at this point, prepared in a calmer and more realistic way than before to meet the clinical demands of their third and final year.

This is an example of when it was difficult for a well-established group to make the transition to reflection on practice, and we decided as facilitators to gently but firmly nudge them towards this rather than to force the issue. My understanding is that at the start of the meeting, anxieties about starting the final year of training, largely in response to unrealistically high expectations of themselves as 'senior trainees', were getting in the way of a grounded engagement with clinical work. Hopefully, Miranda and I did some useful work in helping the trainees to process these anxieties. They were then able to acknowledge all they had learned and to reflect on what they had to offer clients as they embarked on their final year placements, and to show a readiness for new therapeutic relationships.

Techniques

It is fairly common for groups to have a check-in at the start of meetings, going around the group and inviting each member to say how they are. This can be a useful way of beginning a group meeting, allowing time and space for connections between members to re-form in a more personal way than is usual in busy work settings. A check-in can work well if the group organises it efficiently, with most members making fairly minimal contributions and people talking at greater length when there is a need. But a check-in can take too long, and risks introducing an issue into the group which it either cannot address properly or diverts its focus from reflection on practice. It can also put group members on the spot, forcing them to say something when they might not wish to do so. I have facilitated groups when a member has spoken about a painful personal issue during a check-in, leaving the group with a dilemma as to whether to risk insensitivity and move on to the planned generation of material from practice, or focus its attention on a suffering colleague. Of course, there are times when tending to the personal needs of a colleague is absolutely the right thing to do. But a regular, systematic check-in may introduce personal experiences into a reflective practice group more often than is helpful.

My preference is for a general check-in, in which I ask how things are, aiming to take, metaphorically speaking, the temperature of the room. If this approach is working, colleagues will talk about immediate agitations or concerns for five or ten minutes, and will bring up something more individual if they feel it is relevant to do so. I see it as my responsibility to help the group turn in to its reflective task after a few minutes, or a bit longer if we need it, although groups usually get used to doing this automatically. It feels as if with a more general check-in of this sort we are able to acknowledge the state of mind and body in which people enter the room, hearing about preoccupations which feel as if they might get in the way of reflective practice, and do a bit of processing together to help put them to one side.

I have been a member of a successful reflective practice group in which the facilitator did little to enable a transition to reflexivity apart from communicating a clear expectation that the group would focus on its task from the start, and embodying a serious and thoughtful mode in their manner and way of being. I think what happens in these instances is that the feel of the group, by which I mean both the physical atmosphere of the setting and the manner in which the facilitator relates to the group and in which group members relate to each other, become associations or markers that enable a transition to take place to reflective mode.

I have also heard from facilitators of reflective practice groups who use a mindfulness exercise to reduce the power of external preoccupations and bring members into the here and now. This is usually a one- to three-minute exercise which promotes a keen and focused awareness of immediate physical sensations and mental experience (Williams & Penman, 2011). Group members look at what is going on inside themselves, which brings a sense of distance and perspective to pressures and concerns, thus reducing their impact. Such techniques will be most useful to those practitioners who are familiar with them because they already use them in their practice. The members of one group I know about chose to use a range of mindfulness exercises in this way, coming to an arrangement whereby the responsibility for leading the exercise rotated around the group, and they did similar but different exercises each time.

The disadvantage of introducing a mindfulness technique at the Turning In stage is that individuals are left to cope with external stresses and preoccupations on their own, when it might be helpful to make links between such concerns and whatever emerges during the group at the more detailed clinical practice level. In the preceding illustration, my co-facilitator and I thought that general anxiety about entering the final year of training was connected with difficulty in engaging with material relating to individual clients. If we had used a mindfulness exercise to help members make the transition, the shift may have been achieved more efficiently, but we could not have made the link explicit and learnt from it in the way we did.

Table 4.1 Pros and cons of different techniques for Turning In

Approach or technique	*Pros and cons*
Systematic check-in involving each group member	Helps group connect with each other and put aside external concerns; can take too long, put people on the spot and introduce material which diverts from the group task
Open, more general check-in	The group can process external concerns if and when necessary; relies on members feeling sufficiently safe to talk about pressures from outside when relevant
Immediate focus on reflective practice task; setting and approach of facilitator become markers of transition	Efficient, no time wasted; facilitator and group need to be able to make the transition, so this may work less well if there are pressing and ongoing external issues with which members are struggling
Use of an exercise, for example, a mindfulness technique	Good way of achieving focus for those familiar with these exercises, but the group does not have the opportunity to learn about or deal with relevant external issues

Key influence

Since the 1990s, brain imaging techniques have revolutionised neuroscience and our approach to the physiology of mind. Bessel van der Kolk's book *The Body Keeps the Score: Mind, Brain and Body in the Transformation of Trauma* introduced me to recent research into the way the brain and body react to traumatic stress. It seems highly relevant to what I observe in healthcare staff attending reflective practice groups, and particularly, to transition points in the group process such as the Turning In stage. Distinctly traumatic experiences of the sort which directly threaten your physical safety or the safety of those you love are not a regular part of NHS clinical practice. However, lower-level traumatic events, and particularly, exposure to the trauma of others and the consequent risk of being affected vicariously, is a regular part of the job. Healthcare staff frequently experience what I would describe as low-level traumatic stress, particularly when services are very overstretched.

Van der Kolk describes the way in which heightened stress activates the parts of the mind and body involved in defensive action and deactivates those parts which generate creative and relational thinking – the resources we aim to draw on in reflective practice (van der Kolk, 2014). These different aspects to mind and body are quite separate and distinct, and moving from one to another is clearly a physical as well as a mental transition. He also gives an account of the difficulty that traumatised individuals have in regaining a sense of physical safety once any threat has been removed, and the way in which people can become trapped in, and even addicted to, stressful and high-impact experiences. I think we see something of this in the difficulty that pressured healthcare staff have in finding time for reflective practice and, once they have got to a group, in turning into it and entering the reflective mode.

Van der Volk also describes three basic physiological states in response to high stress: the first is one in which we instinctively seek help and comfort from those around us, as happens in a reflective practice group; the second, which kicks in if there is no effective help available, is the fight or flight response; and the third, which takes over if escape from the situation is not possible, is a collapsed or frozen state. This latter state, in which the body is often somewhat numbed and the mind disconnected, is akin to the burnout which we know is widespread amongst overworked healthcare workers (Monsalve-Reyes et al., 2018). These findings provide an explanation for why it is hard for healthcare staff under stress to gear down immediately the opportunity to do so is offered to them, and why it is important to work with staff to help them make the transition to a more relaxed and relational mode.

Summary

- The Turning In stage involves the transition from a busy, pressured and active work mode to a thoughtful and reflective one; this can feel like a difficult shift to make because staff are often working in very stressful environments and are naturally anxious about opening up about their practice in front of colleagues.
- Research into the biology of the body's stress response helps us understand why the shift can be a hard one to make, since the active, defensive mode we go into is not easy to get out of if we are in a situation of acute or ongoing stress.
- Recent findings from neuroscience show that when under stress, the parts of the brain which allow for empathy, linguistic communication and high-level emotional processing are deactivated; from a clinical point of view, as well as for the sake of staff well-being, it is, therefore, important to provide time and space to think in a calm and nonreactive way about the complexities of healthcare work.
- Sometimes, staff attending a reflective practice group do not make the transition from preoccupation with service issues to a reflective mode; it can be tempting for the facilitator to go along with this, particularly if they are internal to the organisation; but if it goes on for too long or happens often, staff can become frustrated and feel they are missing out.
- Alternatively the group may enter fairly quickly into reflection on practice, but the stressed and preoccupied state of those attending may have a strong but hidden effect, limiting members' capacity to fully engage with the material presented; this should be sensitively addressed by the facilitator in case it is possible to help reduce the constraining effect of external pressures.
- Techniques for enabling the transition to a reflective mode include: moving straight into a focus on reflective practice, which can work when the group knows what it is doing and the facilitator confidently embodies the reflective approach; a systematic check-in in which each member (including the facilitator) says something about how they are before starting the group, or a general check-in in which members take a little time to talk about something pressing if needed but do not go around the group one-by-one.

- Mindfulness exercises are increasingly popular as a way of enabling the transition to a reflective mode: they can be a useful way of changing gear, but they do not allow for exploration of connections between preoccupations with organisational issues and experiences at the clinical level, nor of the extent to which individual concerns are shared.

References

Freeman, D. & Freeman, J. (2012) *Anxiety: a very short introduction*. Oxford: Oxford University Press.

Monsalve-Reyes, C.S., San Luis-Costas, C., Gomez-Urquiza, J.L., Albendin-Garcia, L., Aguayo, R. & Canadas-De La Fuente, G.A. (2018) Burnout syndrome and its prevalence in primary care nursing: a systematic review and meta-analysis. *BMC Family Practice*, 19(1): 59.

Norcross, J. (Ed.) (2011) *Psychotherapy relationships that work: evidence-based responsiveness* (2nd ed.). Oxford: Oxford University Press.

Solomon, R.L. (1980) The opponent-process theory of acquired motivation: the costs of pleasure and the benefits of pain. *American Psychologist*, 35: 691–712.

van der Kolk, B. (2014) *The body keeps the score: mind, brain and body in the transformation of trauma*. London: Penguin Books.

van der Kolk, B. (1989) The compulsion to repeat the trauma: re-enactment, revictimization and masochism. *Psychiatric Clinics of North America*, 12(2): 389–411.

Williams, M. & Penman, D. (2011) *Mindfulness: a practical guide to finding peace in a frantic world*. London: Piatkus Books.

5 Looking Back

What is Looking Back?

Looking Back is the stage when the group gives space for reflections in response to previous meetings, following up on thoughts which may have occurred after the last meeting or in response to meetings before then. During this stage the presenter from last time may have more to say about suggestions from the group and how these have or have not connected with their practice; they may feel better able to express a doubt or articulate a question than they were at the time, or something from the discussion may have made sense to them when they went back into the practice situation in a way they did not anticipate. They, or other members of the group, may want to return to something which they are curious about, or which it seems important to explore further.

The Looking Back stage exists in recognition of the fact that the development of reflective practice takes time and occurs in relation to the lived experience of work, rather than only through reflective discussion. The process should be an iterative one, in which reflection shapes and modifies practice, and in turn, what happens in interactions outside the group with clients and colleagues informs thinking within the group. It is useful at this stage to explore the nature of the influence of reflection on practice since it can be unclear how the ideas generated by discussion will influence the clinical situation, and how experience in the work situation will then impact upon the way in which members think about the activity of the group. Reflective practice can play a significant part in altering the meaning which group members attribute to a clinical situation or interaction over time, and it can be useful for the group to share in these transformative moments.

It often simply takes time for thoughts and feelings about difficult and complex areas of clinical practice to come together and take shape. Reflective practice does not necessarily produce results quickly or in the space of a single meeting. Indeed, one of the functions of the Looking Back stage is to provide a check on the strong impulse to master the understanding of an issue each time the group meets, or to start afresh at the beginning of each meeting – whether or not there are interesting and important discussions to follow up on. The Looking Back stage provides the structure for a process of fluid and ongoing learning and the space to follow through on a line of thinking. Much of the time just a few minutes will be needed to hear about responses to a previous meeting. But sometimes there is more to work on, and it is best if the group can either give time to whatever has emerged there and then, or allocate proper time to it at a future meeting.

A key aim of this stage is to allow space for processing of clinical experiences and interactions; these are often complex and high in their emotional impact, and making sense of them takes distance and mental effort. Healthcare practitioners are the recipients of the emotional communications of clients and colleagues, and the group can play a valuable role in raising awareness of feelings and giving meaning to interactions. When those using healthcare services are in emotional and physical pain they often struggle with feelings of vulnerability, rage, fear and so on. It may not be possible for them to deal in a conscious way with what is going on, but they may well communicate what they are feeling to those in close contact with them – partly as a way of getting rid of difficult emotions and partly in the hope of being understood (Casement, 2014).

This means, for example, that the nurse of a patient who is terrified, but unable to know about their fear, may find themselves feeling unaccountably anxious, while their patient remains rather blasé and detached. Or the psychologist working with a client who feels vulnerable and got at, but cannot admit this to themselves, may find themselves on the receiving end of attacking behavior, leading them to feel intimidated by their client and unable to engage properly as a therapist. These emotional communications, which are brought about through subtle interactions and often remain outside of conscious awareness, are brought to the reflective practice group, and the perspectives of colleagues help to untangle what is going on, and whose feelings belong to whom. This is a kind of working through, which draws on the personal resources of group members and takes time and space to make use of retrospective consideration, as members make sense of what is spoken about in relation to their lived experiences inside and outside the group.

Through the creation of a space to which the ripple effects of reflective practice can be brought, the Looking Back stage aims to modify the pressure reflective practice groups can put on themselves to master unique and complex situations too completely and too quickly. Facilitators have often told me that they feel they should know the answer to the question put before the group and find themselves attempting to offer a solution by the end of each group, whether they feel they actually have one or not. They describe working hard in the privacy of their own minds to construct a full psychological formulation of a case, as if it is expected that they should produce this for the benefit of the group. Sometimes the group seems to demand expert instruction from the facilitator, bringing a fresh problem each time, which is discussed by all but is ultimately the facilitator's job to solve. Sometimes the facilitator may impose this demand upon themselves. Either way, the Looking Back stage functions to relieve this pressure and to create a realistic working pace for the group as a whole.

Nowadays the expectation that results will be achieved quickly is perhaps especially pronounced. John Tomlinson in his book *The Culture of Speed: The Coming of Immediacy* has described the last twenty years as an age of immediacy, a time in which digital technologies have developed to offer a level of connectedness that appears to shrink the globe and allow transactions, in business and beyond, to take place almost instantaneously (Tomlinson, 2007). Ours is a time in which the limits of time and space seem sometimes to have disappeared altogether. So also, in our era of connectedness, have boundaries between people. We are able to form relationships and communities on social media quickly, identifying areas of common interest and experience at the click of a mouse. There can be an illusion that we actually know and understand these people with whom we connect. But, as Tomlinson reminds us, the new technologies partly work on the basis of the illusion of connectedness, and there are costs to forgetting what is real in our digital interactions and what is not. It is also likely that experiences of immediacy in digital relationships influence expectations of how quickly we can connect with people in the non-digital realm. If we are not careful we may grow intolerant of the real work and time involved in knowing about and caring for other people, particularly those who are in trouble or suffering.

Table 5.1 The aims of the Looking Back stage with examples

Why do it?	Example
To track links between reflection in the group and experience of practice outside the group, learning about the impact of group discussions in the clinical situation and vice versa	A colleague who brought a case is taking things in at the end of the group and not able to say much about what they make of the responses of others; at the next meeting, they can report on ideas they found useful and want to follow up on and responses which feel less relevant
To modify and counter the pressure for speed and mastery, and the idea that discussion in the group should be wrapped up and something new presented each time the group meets	Towards the end of a group there is a feeling of heaviness, which makes it difficult to think (as in the Illustration in the Turning Out chapter); rather than struggling to offer a formulation, the facilitator and members notice and comment upon this, and at the Looking Back stage next time people have thoughts to share about how they understand the heavy feeling in the context of the material presented to the group
To follow up on issues which have emerged, supporting a process whereby the group has time and space to work something through	A previous discussion, which yielded initial thoughts about how to understand difficult feelings towards a client, has had an emotional impact on the group; they found the discussion helpful but would like to go over it again, linking it to the experiences of other members and consolidating their learning
To give opportunities to learn about the ripple effects of reflective practice over time	A colleague says they are finding it difficult to get alongside their client, and discussion in the group promotes understanding of interactions between the practitioner and client by making links with the client's history; sometime later, the colleague reports how after the group they felt more empathic towards the client and over time this opened up new areas of exploration in therapy

Critical issues

The Looking Back stage tends to be missed out or included in a routine way as only a brief review of the last meeting of the group, as opposed to a proper space to follow up on work when this is what is needed. It is useful to keep this stage brief in the normal run of things (say five minutes long), because this leaves plenty of time for new material to be generated for the group. In my experience this works most of the time, as long as space is given to see an issue through more fully when this is required. Members will often feel unable to use the stage in this way, particularly early on, so it may be up to the facilitator to remind the group of a meaningful previous discussion, or something which was left hanging in the balance. If a member has brought something to share, which they would like help with that day, I suggest splitting the time into two; this is if we have an hour and a half, or at least thirty minutes available for each item. Or I suggest returning to the follow-up discussion next time.

Reflective practice groups, just like any type of clinical supervision, can fall into the trap of a routinised shift of focus at each meeting to a different case or issue, with the implication that a new piece of learning should be undertaken every time. In my experience it is helpful for members to bring experiences to reflective practice to share regularly, particularly as reluctance to do this is generally more of a problem than the opposite. However, it is helpful if the group can be flexible in the pace of learning it adopts, giving more time to issues, which members find difficult, or which need longer to integrate into their experience.

The routinised approach runs the risk of opening up areas of curiosity and difficulty without allowing the group to achieve a satisfactory solution or resolution. Complete answers cannot always be found in reflective practice, but it is usually possible to deepen understanding of complex problems if a process, such as the one outlined in the Intersubjective Model, is followed through. On the other hand, the facilitator may feel a strong demand to wrap up the group's learning each time, providing a solution to a problem posed, or an answer to a question. There are a number of difficulties with the facilitator going along with this pressure too often. It positions them as the expert who has the answers, reducing opportunities for the group to build up resources of its own. It also distracts the facilitator from the task of group facilitation: if you are busy trying to find a solution to a complex and ambiguous problem, you are probably not focusing as well as you could on drawing out the responses of group members, helping them to discover what they think and feel, and encouraging the articulation of their responses and associations. To some extent, there is a choice between offering expert instruction and facilitating a group process, and in a reflective practice group the latter should not be sacrificed to the former – at least not for long.

In addition over-quick mastery of problems by the group and expert instruction by the facilitator, provide an unrealistic model for practitioners of the resolution of unique and complex clinical problems. In-depth understanding of knotty clinical issues is certainly possible in a reflective practice group, but not without putting in time and effort, and not without going back to things at least some of the time. The Looking Back stage promotes resilience in healthcare staff through supporting persistence in the face of difficulty, and the generation of real solutions, rather than superficial ones, by the group working together through areas of confusion and difficulty.

Illustration: a trainee clinical psychologist looks back at how her identity as a clinician has changed during the course of a reflective practice group

I am going to use material from a research interview to show the value of looking back on the process of learning in a reflective practice group. The interview was carried out as part of an in-depth study into how participation in a reflective practice group impacted the way trainee clinical psychologists thought about their clients and their emerging identities as practitioner psychologists. Anya Biggins (2019) was a member of the group and carried out the research; I co-facilitated the group and also acted as the academic supervisor. As participant-researchers it was important for Anya and me to think carefully about our position in relation to the research, and to ensure that we were as open as possible to experiences of the group which did not fit with our own. There were six trainees in the group, which lasted for three years of training.

Anya taped monthly meetings of the group for the first two years of training. She selected two short excerpts for each group member, one from when they presented a case in the first year of training and the other from when they presented a case in the second year. Anya played both excerpts during the interviews in order to prompt discussion about experiences of the reflective practice group over time.

In one interview a trainee called Helen said that, overall, the experience of the reflective practice group had had a 'big impact' on how she thought about clients; in the clinical situation, she sometimes found herself automatically bringing to mind the way other members of the group thought about their work with clients and colleagues. Helen reflected on her experience of sharing a case in the group for the first time, and how unsure she felt about what to talk about and what to leave out. She spoke about how frustrated she was in her work with a client who had ostensibly come for help with one problem but talked all the time about something else, and who took control of the sessions, leaving little space for Helen to contribute. Helen usually felt compassionate towards her clients; but at the moment, she did not feel this way towards this particular client, and she did not understand why this was. Others in the group responded with curiosity about the client's history, and as they learnt more, they made observations about how successful the client was at keeping others at a distance. One member of the group conveyed this vividly through an image of the client as someone small and vulnerable who was wearing great big boxing gloves, and was busy fighting people off.

In the interview Helen recalled initially finding it difficult that she had shared feelings of frustration and yet others were able to empathise with the client. At the time of the seminar, she felt critical of herself, and as if she had failed because of her emotional response. Helen said: 'there was a right story and a wrong story and everyone else had given the right story, that's kind of what it felt like then'.

She went on to say that she did not think of the interactions in the seminar in the same way now: she felt less critical of herself, and more compassionate, and she considered how helpful the different perspectives of others had been in developing a fuller understanding of the client, and how this had impacted on therapeutic work. This is how Helen put it:

> Yeah listening back to it now I was thinking 'God I really took that to heart, I really took that as really personal feedback on how I was doing and now I . . . think 'You know what, that was really helpful' and I can understand why I didn't have a similar picture of her in a compassionate way because actually being in it was really difficult . . . I was coming at it from a different point from the rest of the group because I was so in it and they were able to take that step back . . . after I came back from reflective practice it's like another sort of filter had been put in those lenses like another lens on top, so I was seeing her through both my initial feelings towards her but also the group's reflections of her . . . because I could see her differently I, in turn, responded to her differently which I think led us to different things in the therapy . . .

Helen describes a shift from a relatively narrow approach to thinking about clinical work, in which there is just a right and a wrong answer, to one in which it is possible to make use of multiple positions and perspectives within a group in order to build a more complex picture of what is happening. The learning field has become wider and richer, and this is something that has happened for Helen over some period of time. This is to be expected as reflective practice is a form of learning which takes place across situations through an iterative process of thinking and doing. It is helpful during the Looking Back stage to have a space to capture this process, thereby consolidating learning within the group.

Key influences

Psychoanalytic theory about unconscious communication, and particularly the concept of projective identification, has shaped my approach to the Looking Back stage. Patrick Casement (1985) gives a full and clear account of this in his book *On Learning from the Patient*. He explains how disowned feelings are communicated to others in an impactful but disguised way, with which others, such as colleagues in a supervision or reflective practice group, can help. Their distance from the interaction, the fact that they are not in the midst of it, allows them to see and notice things which those directly involved are less aware of. When a person feels something which they find difficult to acknowledge or own as part of their own experience, they will often deal with it by placing it in someone else – thinking of another person as angry rather than themselves, or as vulnerable and weak, or as proud and capable, when they themselves do not feel this way (even though they are). It is important to note that people often disown positive as well as negative feelings and qualities. If the person on the receiving end of the communication is receptive, they are likely to experience the disowned feeling, usually because they have been treated in a way which invites them to feel something, but in a subtle or even a hidden way.

Colleagues in a reflective practice group may well be able to see how a disowned feeling is being covered up or disguised in the way the client is behaving, and to connect with this feeling and bring it back to the practitioner to integrate into their clinical understanding. But in my experience, it takes time as well as distance to unravel emotions in this type of situation, which is where the Looking Back stage comes in. It is not enough to grasp what is going on in intellectual terms. The power of unconscious communication is experienced in the practice situation when engagement with the client deepens as a result of knowledge gained in the group, or when it becomes clear that more work needs to be done in shaping this knowledge.

We live in an age which places a high value on speed and on immediate gratification. The Looking Back stage acts to some extent as a brake, emphasising as it does the time it takes to process discussions about the complexities of clinical practice and to integrate abstract elements with experience in developing healthcare practice. John Tomlinson's book *The Culture of Speed: The Coming of Immediacy* has been a useful reference, describing the subtle and not-so-subtle expectations of immediacy shaped by digital technologies and the potential costs of these. Tomlinson articulates two narratives in the history of the Western world since the Industrial Revolution. The first he names 'machine speed', which is the triumphant story of the way in which humans overtook nature through the invention of machines, such as the railways, which were quicker and more powerful than anything that had gone before. The second, which relates to the rise of digital technologies in the past twenty years, is called the age of immediacy. It describes the sense of presence and immediacy created by the instant connectedness of our new technologies. This is enhanced by the use of sound and touch in operating them, and the impression they create of literally breaking down barriers of time and place. The fact that I can communicate virtually instantaneously, and at the sound of my voice or the touch of my finger, with colleagues around the world does seem magical.

However Tomlinson reminds us that this experience of instant connection has a significant illusory aspect. I can get a message to someone on the other side of the world incredibly quickly and easily, but this is not the same as being together and getting to know each other in real space and time, even if it feels the same. It is likely to be an inadequate way of communicating about difficult and complex feelings and reactions of the sort our clients bring to us. Of course, we do not use digital technologies in our interactions with clients a great deal yet (although this is on the increase). But I do wonder whether there is a risk that a growing expectation of immediacy in communications is making us less patient in our relationships, and in human services, less able to give time and effort to work at issues involving subtlety, complexity and challenge. We need to ensure that we do not neglect the development of slower and more in-depth approaches in healthcare, bringing them into use alongside fast-paced, technological methods and learning more about how to make the two work in an integrated way.

Summary

- The Looking Back stage allows space for follow-through, for the presenter from the previous meeting to respond when they have had time to process the discussion and test ideas out in the practice situation, and for the group to continue thinking about an issue which needs more time.
- This stage allows for members to reflect on the learning process in the group as it unfolds, and thereby gives the opportunity for sharing experiences of the ripple effects created by a reflective practice group in the clinical situation.
- It should be possible to bring reflections either from the last meeting or from previous meetings to the Looking Back stage.
- This stage aims to provide an ongoing structure for the process of developing understanding over time, and so to check the impulse, either in the facilitator or the group as a whole, towards unrealistic speed and mastery of the understanding of complex conundrums and human situations in a one-off group discussion.
- This stage is often missed out altogether or included as a routine check back to the previous meeting; it is helpful to have such a check, but also to be flexible in allowing time to follow through in working out a problem or going over a difficult area, either when this comes up or by allocating a future meeting for this purpose.
- The psychoanalytic theory of unconscious communication has been influential in developing this stage because it shows clearly the mental work involved in processing high-impact emotions in the clinical situation, and the value of being able to test ideas out in practice and then go over them again with supportive colleagues to shape and deepen understanding.

References

Biggins, A. (2019) *Does group reflective practice change practitioners' understanding of clients? An Interpretative Phenomenological Analysis of the impact of monthly reflective practice groups within clinical psychology training.* Unpublished Dissertation; University of Leicester.

Casement, P. (2014, first published in 1985) *On learning from the patient.* London: Routledge Mental Health Classic Editions.

Tomlinson, J. (2007) *The culture of speed: the coming of immediacy.* London: Sage Publications Inc.

6 Generation

What is the Generation stage?

The Generation stage is when a member of the group produces material relating to their practice for reflective consideration by their colleagues. This may be a clinical case – indeed, it is useful for the focus to be on ground level clinical work since this can sometimes get lost. Or it may be another, more general, issue from practice, such as the way in which a referrals meeting runs or the approach of the service to medication or discharge. What is important is that material is brought in a way which allows for fruitful engagement by the group, something which is made difficult if what is brought is too abstract or closed, in the sense of its meaning having already been decided.

This is an important foundational stage, and is crucial in setting up any reflective activity properly: after all, how can a reflective practice group get going without something from practice to reflect upon? It is, therefore, perhaps, surprising how resistant groups can be to generating material in this way. This is largely, I think, the result of an unhelpful preoccupation with risk in healthcare services, and the constant pressure staff feel to demonstrate professional competence, which results in them wanting, if at all possible, to avoid scrutiny. Defensive practice, so-called, is very much part of the culture of modern healthcare, and staff often need help in reflective practice groups in talking in a less inhibited and rule-bound way about their work in order to bring a question or problem or conundrum to colleagues in such a way as to enable reflective engagement with it.

I have called this stage Generation, rather than the more usual term Presentation. There are two reasons for this. The first is to avoid, as far as possible, an association with the pressure to perform and to demonstrate competence, which are strongly linked with the word presentation. The second is to make explicit the fact that there is an active process of selection and construction involved in the apparently simple matter of presenting the material. Data is actively generated, brought into being in some way or another, rather than simply and passively put before a group.

When we talk of bringing something to a group, bringing, for example, an individual client to talk about, it makes it sounds as if it is just a matter of carrying something in from outside. But if we have learned from the postmodernist tradition, we should hold onto an awareness of the power to create reality – particularly the reality of human problems and relationships. There is no single, true way of representing the clinical issue we might want to discuss in a reflective practice group, even if the professional discourses surrounding us are used in a way which implies much of the time that such matters are givens. The medium we use – whether it is the written or spoken word – is not a straightforward route whereby a fixed and knowable thing that exists in the world is reached. Instead, it is part of creating the world, certainly the world as we know and experience it, part of giving it form and meaning; and this is particularly the case in mental health services, which are so dependent on relationships between people, and on the power of subjective and inter-subjective experience.

So the material we present when we bring our work before colleagues in a reflective practice group is inevitably constructed – selected and shaped in one of many possible ways – and it is important for facilitators and group members to be mindful of how the type of material presented to the group, and the way it is offered or shared, will determine what the group is able to do with it. To some extent, as the saying goes, the output is only as good as the input. For this reason, facilitators need to retain a sense of the main aims of reflective practice at this stage, and to encourage members over time to bring material that fits with these aims.

According to the Intersubjective Model, groups are invited to develop thinking outside of the professional box, taking in their clients not just as clients but as people in a relational context, drawing on the creative and intellectual resources of group members, and finding space to acknowledge emotional responses to the human work that they do, and to give such responses meaning. This means that during the Generation stage of the model, group members should be encouraged to put before the group material which is conducive to reflective practice in a general sense, but with a focus on opening up thinking in comparatively emotional, intuitive and creative ways. After they have done this, their colleagues will have the opportunity to ask questions to fill out the material.

How can we develop an approach to the generation of material during this stage which is informed by these core aims of reflective practice? First and foremost, the purpose of a reflective practice group is to think about the material presented to it in a way which is genuinely helpful. For this reason, it is important that group members feel safe enough to bring real, lived experience of work and genuine questions and problems to the group, as opposed to generating material in such a way that these are smoothed over or covered up.

Research into the effectiveness of clinical supervision, which is limited but growing, supports a focus on safety and trust in relationships in all types of supervision. As Beinart and Clohessy (2017) describe in their book *Effective Supervisory Relationships: Best Evidence and Practice*, a key finding across studies on effective supervision is that the supervisory relationship is absolutely pivotal to positive outcomes. But there is not only one kind of successful supervisory relationship: different kinds of supervisor and supervisory relationship suit different supervisees. So flexibility and the ability of the supervisor to adjust their approach to the individual supervisee's learning style is likely to be significant in determining the outcome. When supervisees are less rather than more satisfied with the supervisory relationship, they tend also to be less confident about their practice, and also less willing to disclose areas of difficulty and uncertainty (Ladany, Mori & Mehr, 2013; Ladany et al., 1996).

If we apply these findings to reflective practice in a group setting, the relationships in the group – both between group members and between the facilitator and the group – will be important in determining whether members feel able to bring real problems and dilemmas for the group to reflect on. The facilitator will need to be alive to members' feelings of safety and trust in the environment of the group as a whole, and also to their experience of the group process as helpful and purposeful. This will come partly as the result of a connection between the way in which material is generated at this stage and what the group is able to do with it later on.

The association for many with the word presentation is with a relatively formal talk, usually accompanied by overheads. This type of presentation usually has the purpose of informing, instructing or entertaining the audience, and also, implicitly, of demonstrating the skills and competence of the presenter. It involves an element of performance, and is often accompanied by some measure of anxiety about opening oneself up to the judgement of others. In the reflective practice context, we are not after this kind of presentation but something more open and considerably less finished. But I think it is naïve to assume that we can move towards a different kind of presentation without first acknowledging the influence of the idea of a presentation as a demonstration of competence. Its shadow often lurks not far behind the presentations of staff who come to reflective practice groups, particularly if their working environment is felt to be critical and scrutinising.

Such staff will often only have had experience of what is referred to as management supervision, a type of supervision which is primarily designed to check on whether staff are doing a good enough job and to rule out malpractice. In my experience this model of supervision has a formative influence on staff and is strongly internalised by them, and a facilitator of reflective practice will have to work patiently over time to introduce a more explorative way of talking and thinking about clinical work.

At the Generation stage, a comparatively informal and open approach to producing material for the group should be encouraged. This does not mean that the material produced should be scanty or thin – in fact, quite the opposite. Members are invited to bring the rich detail of lived experience to the reflective practice group, letting colleagues know about their thoughts and impressions in as full and expansive a way as possible. Hopefully, in time, they will be able to do this relatively spontaneously because they will learn that in so doing they convey a fuller and more real sense of their experience of clinical practice, of the person or people they are engaging with and of themselves in the work, and of how they are feeling about it and what it is that they are finding confusing or difficult. What I have found, however, is that this more spontaneous and apparently unstructured method of generating data is deceptive in its simplicity. Facilitators often need to put quite a bit of effort early on into making their expectations of what will be covered at this stage explicit, and providing some scaffolding so that group members have a sense of how to make the transition from a familiar and relatively structured account of their practice to one that is open and allows for explorative investigation by the group.

It is usually best to start with an emphasis on cases, since this is a familiar model of presentation for healthcare staff, and it makes it easier for them to learn about a new way of generating clinical material for the purposes of reflective practice. It is helpful if group members bring the sort of material that usually forms part of an assessment, such as: the presenting difficulty, background information about the problem and the client's referral to the service, the client's history and other relevant information necessary to help the group get a good understanding of the work issue in the normal way. Medics will have

Table 6.1 How to get the Generation stage started

Getting started: areas to cover	Emphasis: the how not the what
Description of client, including presenting problem, referral pathway, history and other relevant information	Focus on the difficulty as client sees it rather than more objective description, and on the history and development of client, including aspects other than the defined problem
Human detail, sense of what client is like	Encourage practitioner to explore impressions and feelings
Material about interactions with client and their relationships, including relationship with the practitioner	As above, but moving outwards a bit to consider ways in which people tend to respond to client
Sense of why colleague is generating material for group: what is the question, problem or feeling to be explored?	This is a useful touchpoint for the group; it may or may not be clear, and it is often in its nature to be unclear

their own particular focuses for assessment which they will draw upon here, as will psychologists, nurses, social workers and occupational therapists. However over time presenters should be encouraged to generate material in a less technically abstract, more grounded way than is usually the case in modern healthcare services. The aim is to get close to experience – the client's and the practitioner's – and to move away from professional jargon as part of bringing this about. It is preferable to talk about the difficulty as the client lives it, for example, rather than through the medium of diagnostic or specialist language. In addition, groups should try to expand upon the more traditional type of assessment material because, for the purposes of reflective practice, the group needs to hear about the more messy, human and relational aspects of the situation.

Areas that members could be encouraged to explore are: the sense of the client as a person – how they strike the practitioner and what impressions and feelings the practitioner has about them; the client's history and development, including a sense of their interests and activities, making sure to widen the focus out from their problems; the quality of their relationships and the sense of the practitioner in relation to the client, something that often comes to life in the group as the practitioner starts to give words to experiences in the clinical situation; and, last but not least, the question or problem, which underlies the practitioner's decision to bring the material before the group and is often by its nature unclear or half-formed. For example, they may be preoccupied with something which has happened with one of their clients but not know why; or they may find it difficult to get a client or colleague out of their minds but be puzzled as to why this is.

It can be difficult for practitioners to start to talk in this less guarded, more explorative way about clients and their problems. It can even feel somewhat unprofessional and irresponsible. I remember years ago being shocked at the judgemental way in which some medical colleagues tended to write about patients in letters and reports, describing them as, for example, 'young, attractive and female' or 'overweight and middle-aged'. This seemed symptomatic of a patriarchal, moralising strand within the medical establishment, and it was something we were keen as developing professionals to get away from.

In a reflective practice group, however, the context for honest naming of reactions is altogether different. There is a clinical rationale for encouraging staff to open up in this way, which is that we all have emotional responses to the human work we do, even if we keep these responses within the privacy of our own minds, and we are more likely to act on them in an unhelpful way if they remain unacknowledged and, therefore, unavailable for thought and understanding. What this means is that staff should be able to explore such feelings in a safe, confidential space in which they can be processed, rather than taken as a static and complete view of the client. What is spoken about in this way in reflective practice should be kept within the group and the identity of clients and group members should be firmly protected so that reactions can be used for thinking about clinical work, rather than as gossip or criticism.

Critical issues from practice

Reluctance on the part of group members to talk in an open and detailed way about practice is the most common difficulty facilitators encounter in making the transition to the Generation stage. In my experience this takes the form of group members saying they have nothing to bring (although, as in the illustration in the following section, if one scratches the surface this is rarely the case), or being disorganised with regards to any plan for who will present and when. It can also emerge as opposition in the group to a structure which is seen as an unnecessary constraint imposed by the facilitators. Members will speak about all the varied and interesting issues they would like to discuss, expressing the desire to get away from what is represented as a rigid or boring focus on cases. It is a positive development, in my view, when a reflective practice group becomes wide-ranging in its scope,

Table 6.2 Reflective practice aims and consequent approaches to generating material

Reflective practice aim	Implication for the material brought at the Generation stage
To share experience of practice with colleagues in order to get their input Vs. to instruct or demonstrate competence	Informal Vs. formal presentation of material
As above	Open Vs. closed and presented as done and dusted
To bring the experience to life for colleagues and allow them to have their own thoughts and responses to it	As rich as possible, grounded in concrete detail, uncontrolled
To give a vivid account, inviting listeners to relate to material and have feeling responses	A focus on human interest and relationships
To be open to colleague's thoughts about presenter's position in relation to the material generated	A focus on relationship with client(s) and colleagues in practice situation

taking in something of the range of the activities and experiences with which group members are involved. But there is a difference, which facilitators need to be alive to, between curiosity-driven discussions and talking about anything and everything, as it were, as a way of avoiding looking in-depth at experiences from practice.

Resistance to putting oneself on the line before colleagues and talking openly about clinical work comes from all-too-understandable anxiety about exposure. This is not helped by the nature of the working environment in modern healthcare systems. As an example, the National Health Service in the UK, where I work, has been managed in an increasingly top-down way in recent years, and with this has developed a risk-averse culture, which is highly regulated. Staff can often feel as if they are being scrutinised by their managers, as well as by government and society, and are driven to cover up mistakes, rather than to accept the lower level ones as an aspect of the job, and try to learn from them. In addition recent cuts have made staff anxious about keeping their jobs, increasing their sense that it is necessary to fight for professional survival. When staff come to reflective practice with these sorts of anxieties, it can feel very threatening indeed to be invited to explore the messier areas of clinical practice.

The situation is often a confusing one for healthcare practitioners. On the one hand, managers and senior staff talk about the importance of reflective practice and commissioning of reflective practice groups is on the increase. I do not believe that they are just paying lip-service to its value. Many people in healthcare share the view that having space to think in response to questions and anxieties that come up in the work is integral to the delivery of a high-quality clinical service which looks after its staff. On the other hand, we often practice in healthcare systems that appear to be set up to obstruct open and non-defensive thinking about what we do. This paradox, and the anxiety and confusion that result from it, should be acknowledged and explored by facilitators. The hope is that this will make it easier for members to experience the group as a safe place, separate from the wider organisation, in which to think about their work.

There is another fundamental reason why it is, to some extent, inevitable that staff will feel some anxiety about sharing details of their practice, and looking at themselves in their relationships with clients. This relates to the intimate nature of the clinical situation, and the way it brings staff into close contact with human suffering and vulnerability. In these relationships, staff have the power to heal and hurt and can feel both responsible and anxious about this responsibility at the same time. Menzies Lyth has described how healthcare staff are drawn to the work of caring for those in physical and/or emotional distress for reparative reasons, which are related to their own histories. Therefore their interactions with clients are likely to be significant to them in ways they both know and do not know about (Menzies Lyth, 1960). In my experience clinicians do have strong fantasies about themselves as healers which it can be helpful to begin to look at in reflective practice if one is respectful of personal boundaries. Staff are relieved to discover that colleagues have similar anxieties, and can free themselves from some of the unrealistic pressures they have taken on in the caring role. These discussions also release staff from fantasies they have about the work of other clinicians, which are often distorted. Members have spoken about 'impostor syndrome', the idea that other people are in possession of healing secrets, while they are just getting away with what they are doing and hoping no one will find out or notice.

These fears can mean that the type of material produced at this stage may be rather thin and abstract, or focused exclusively on the client as an individual instead of the network of relationships around the client, including the relationship between the practitioner and the client. It is usual for the material generated early on in a reflective practice group to be framed within the professional language used by the service, focused, for example, on diagnostic labels and risk issues in a forensic setting, or on medical health problems in a primary care setting. Over time the facilitator aims to change this, and if the material generated continues to lack depth and detail they will need to sympathetically but firmly address this.

In many groups members have a common interest or area of practice but work quite separately from each other, which means that it is relatively straightforward for individuals to generate material for reflective consideration and for the material to be understood to belong to them as an individual. In other groups members work together in a service but function autonomously much of the time as, for example, in an outpatient service in which staff have individual caseloads. But in some groups staff work together in a more communal setting, such as a ward, sharing relationships with patients and colleagues. In this situation members will often want to talk as a group about a patient or, having heard a colleague speak about some aspect of their practice, will react from their own experiences of the matter, rather than their perspectives on their colleague's experience.

This can be a problem. The individual who generated material can feel as if they have not been listened to, and a sort of groupthink can start to take hold in which the view is that members should think and feel in the same way about things, and there is no longer a space for the individual contexts for experiences from practice to be looked at. In other words generation of data in a group in this way can be a form of reduction, allowing members to avoid personal ownership of reactions and producing material that is difficult to situate in a specific context. It is helpful if such groups can develop the discipline of generating material from an individual standpoint, even if it relates to a shared experience, and of listening to it in this way. Responses which draw on the common experiences of group members, can come in later, say during the More Effortful Thinking or Turning Out stages, but holding back with these will help the group achieve a sense of focus.

Illustration: a colleague says her supervision group has not been meeting and she has no material to bring to reflective practice, but this turns out not to be the case

I facilitated a group for clinical psychology colleagues working in adult mental health services in a trust in the UK National Health Service, all of whom held posts in community mental health teams. I had been meeting monthly with them for a couple of years to help them think about their supervisory work with multidisciplinary colleagues.

This was an experienced and busy group of colleagues who rarely saw each other at other times, even though they worked for the same

Table 6.3 Advice regarding critical issues at the Generation stage

Critical issues	Summary advice for facilitator
Members are reluctant to bring anything	Acknowledge and explore anxieties about exposure; gently but firmly communicate expectation that the group will work with material brought from practice, setting up a rota if possible
Material is brought but is thin and abstract	Again, acknowledge and explore anxieties about exposure; encourage the generation of material rich in human interest and detail (see Techniques section)
Material is brought but focus is restricted to individual client rather than client's relationships and practitioner's experience of client	Invite curiosity about the details of interactions and relationships, especially the relationship between the client and presenting practitioner
Material is presented which is taken, perhaps prematurely, to relate to shared experience: it belongs to everybody and nobody	Encourage members who work together outside the group to listen to the material generated by a colleague without imposing their own experience on it, or to hold back in doing so

organisation and carried out similar activities. They enjoyed getting together, and it could be difficult to shift them from discussion about general work issues to their supervisory work. They were also somewhat reluctant to organise themselves so that one of them took responsibility for generating material each month, which meant that we had to identify material from practice each time we met. Early on, members had shared their anxiety about being exposed in the group as 'not really doing anything' in their supervisory practice, a worry which we came to understand largely as the result of the chronic undervaluation of psychological work within the organisation as a whole. Although they were skilled supervisors, who were working effectively with multidisciplinary colleagues to develop a psychological understanding of clients and staff-client relationships, they could easily find themselves feeling that what they were offering was insignificant and insubstantial.

On this occasion, after a catch-up, I asked in the usual way who had something from their supervision group for us to think about. Rosie said that her group had not been meeting, so there was nothing to bring. She went on to say, with reference to previous discussions about coming into post and the difficulties of establishing herself in the team, that she had not been feeling confident about her supervisory work with her multidisciplinary colleagues, but had been telling herself not to mind too much. Her clinical psychology colleagues in our group showed an interest in why the supervision group had not been meeting. Rosie said there had been some staff cuts and everyone was busy and felt they could not spare the time to come. She also mentioned that drug problems had been growing in the local community. Staff were feeling overwhelmed by what was going on. Everyone was just trying to get their work done and go home each day.

It felt as if Rosie had an issue that deserved our attention and had begun to generate rich material for our reflective practice session, even though she had started by saying that there was nothing to talk about. In this respect, she was experiencing something similar to her multi-disciplinary colleagues: they felt reluctant to use a reflective space, perhaps because they were overwhelmed by the staff cuts and increased work burdens, and the emergence of difficulties with drugs in the local community. I spoke about how it might be particularly useful for the team to meet to think together about their practice in the context of this new threat and reduced resources. Others picked up on how para-doxical it was that at the very time when Rosie's multidisciplinary col-leagues might especially need leadership, support and coordination, they were unable to use the resource she had provided.

Rosie talked then at some length about the team context and her feelings about the supervisory group. The cuts in staffing had resulted in destabilisation across the team, and meetings had been disrupted so people were working in increasing isolation. The problems in the local community had been felt by staff in the form of some worrying and occasionally threatening incidents with clients, and some staff were now too frightened to go out on home visits. Rosie made an observa-tion about her lack of confidence in the supervisory input she was offering, and spoke about interactions with individual members of the team which had made her feel unsure of herself.

This point, at which the group had a detailed scenario to work with and a sense too of where Rosie was with the scenario, was the end of the Generation stage. Discussion afterwards, in the Free Response and More Effortful Thinking stages, focused on members' feelings of wanting to bolster Rosie and increase her confidence in her expertise as a supervisor, and thoughts about how mixed the messages from the team had been about the value of psychology input. There was also a developing aware-ness of the way in which Rosie had joined with her colleagues in the idea that things were too busy and difficult for the supervision group to meet, and of how helpful it could be if reflective practice was reinstated.

Techniques

To introduce the Generation stage, I usually give some guidance early on in the life of the group as to what sort of material to produce for the purposes of reflective practice, having learnt over the years that keeping things too open can be unhelpful. As we finish talking about the previous reflective practice session (the Looking Back stage), I will ask who has something to bring. Some groups have a rota with a plan for who is to take responsibility for generating material for the group each time. This can work well, particularly if it is possible to swap places with someone else if there is a pressing issue. I suggest the idea of a rota at the beginning of a group, and usually the group then takes responsibility for this. Sometimes groups prefer not to organise themselves in this way but to be more spontaneous in deciding who will present on a particular day. It does not matter, as long as members take responsibility for generating material from practice and take turns so that over time each member participates in bringing something to the group.

As we start I will indicate how much time we have got for this stage. It would be about twenty minutes in an hour-long group (fifteen minutes to generate material and five minutes for questions) and about half an hour in the case of a longer reflective practice session (twenty minutes for the person talking about their experience and ten minutes for questions).

Colleagues and I have used various creative techniques over the years to free up the process of generating material for reflective practice. These are particularly helpful when a group is stuck in a particular way of thinking about clinical work, finding it, for example, difficult to shift away from a narrowly medical way of constructing psychological distress. The move into another form of expression can open up perspectives, allowing access to more intuitive aspects of practitioners' experience. There are as many different ways of doing this as there are creative methods, and facilitators should choose a technique with which they and the group have some affinity. However for the purposes of illustration, I will describe three approaches with which I am familiar. The first is a creative writing task, the second uses approaches from the visual arts, and the third is drama-based.

In the creative writing task, group members are asked to look again at familiar clinical material by incorporating it into some form of narrative: a short story, for example, or notes towards one. In healthcare services we often get used to thinking about the people we work with in limited ways, seeing them as cases or problems rather than three-dimensional human beings. If invited to approach material generated by a clinical colleague from the point of view of a story, as told in a novel or film, members start to imagine the client and their context more fully. The exercise takes time to do properly, perhaps half an hour to an hour, depending on whether participants start to jot down some ideas for a short story or develop their ideas a bit further, and on how much time is given to digest individual responses. To make it manageable I ask members to write the first paragraph or two of a story with ideas about how the story might develop. It may be worth giving the time to a creative exercise like this as a one-off in order to introduce a new way of thinking to the group. Or one can offer narrative ideas to the group without carrying out a formal exercise, with questions like: 'If you were going to write a story about this situation, can you tell us how you would begin? Or 'If the people you are telling us about were characters in a story how would you describe them?' Or 'If you were writing a story about X, what would happen to them?'

I have also used visual techniques, such as inviting people to draw a diagram or an image to describe a situation. I take in paper and pens and say something like: 'We've heard about X and their problems and also a bit about their life and the people around them. Will you have a go at a drawing that says something about how you see things?' You can ask people to draw a timeline as a way of representing a client's history, or a free form drawing to open up thinking about the impressions of group members in response to what they have heard. You can either suggest that members do individual drawings or have a go at a drawing together. The former is helpful if members are feeling anxious about opening up and talking more freely in front of each other, allowing them to share what they choose of the experience of drawing in response to clinical material. The latter is a good way of bringing about a shift in the culture of a reflective practice group, helping members into a more playful mode of generating material. Again, to do this exercise in full takes time, say half an hour. It may be useful to do it once or twice to introduce a new approach to thinking about cases. If the full exercise does not seem necessary or there is not enough time, the facilitator can simply ask the practitioner generating material what image comes to mind when talking about a client.

Alternatively, there is the possibility of a dramatic sculpt, in which group participants form a shape to express their sense of character and of the relationships between characters in the clinical material. This most physical mode of representation, in which members act out parts of the piece they have heard about, even in the form of an initial stance or gesture, brings about an immediate identification with clients and can be a useful way of breaking down barriers in relation to both clients and colleagues. Group members will also use physical expressions or gestures when they are describing experiences and one can show an interest in these, and perhaps think with the group about what is being expressed through their body language. A role play, in which group members take on characters in the material and act out a scene, is an option as well. It encourages group members to engage imaginatively with clients, which is helpful. But it has the potential for the acted characters to become too real for the group, getting in the way of hearing about the client as represented by the presenter. After all, the purpose of the exercise is to get access to the way the client has been taken in by the presenter and group members, rather than to literally bring the client to life.

Key influences

I am grateful to a colleague from India for making me aware of the influence of my work as a qualitative researcher on the Generation

Table 6.4 Creative exercises for the Generation stage

Type of creative exercise	Description of exercise	The lighter version
Creative writing techniques – applying the narrative imagination to the generation of material	Invite group members to use material to write the first paragraph or two of a short story, or to make notes to develop into a novel or film narrative	Ask if the client was a character in a story or film how the practitioner would describe them or what would happen to them
Visual techniques – applying the visual imagination	Invite members either as individuals or in the group to draw people they have heard about; timelines are a useful way of representing development over time	Ask practitioner to come up with an image of the client, or a visual scene involving them
Dramatic techniques – using physical expression and embodied experience	Invite members to form a sculpture of the client and significant others, or to role play a scene inspired by the material generated	Show interest in the expressions practitioners make when describing work experiences; ask practitioners to use an expression or dramatic gesture to encourage expression

stage of the Intersubjective Model. I was talking at a workshop in Delhi about the value for a reflective practice group of material rich in human interest and the messiness of lived experience, and how this provides a foundation for more conceptual work at a later stage. From the floor came the exclamation: 'I see – it's the Phenomenological Model!' I went back to learn more about phenomenology, the philosophical tradition behind one of the key qualitative methods, Interpretative Phenomenological Analysis, with a sense both of pleasure and recognition. These ideas lay underneath what I was saying and doing, and I had not known it.

Merleau-Ponty (2012), in his classic book *The Phenomenology of Perception*, criticises 'the realist prejudice' underlying much scientific thought, or the interpretation of scientific thought, in which an idealised and often highly abstract form of knowledge about the world is mistaken for knowledge of reality. What he means by this is that if we leave the human subject out of our understanding of what knowledge we generate and how we do this, we make the mistake of assuming that we are discovering real things about the world, rather than actively creating our sense of the world in ways which are powerfully determined by our perceptual and sensual apparatus. Merleau-Ponty considers this 'unquestioned belief in the world' as an obstruction to a deeper form of knowledge, which is based on an acknowledgement of the relationship between subject and object, between the thinking and feeling human subject and their biological, relational and environmental context.

Merleau-Ponty remains very much an empiricist in advocating engagement with 'facticity', by which he means the stuff and detail and rawness of lived experience. This experience always involves a subject and an object, and in Merleau-Ponty's scheme of things, subject and object are in a fluid and constant relation, which he describes as Being-in-the-World. The lived experience of being in the world is, in his view, the foundation of real knowledge, and if we move away from it too quickly into a form of abstract objectification we narrow our field of vision tremendously. We achieve, some of the time at least, a certain clarity and even simplicity, but at the expense of a more nuanced and fuller picture of things.

He writes:

> Reflection does not withdraw from the world to the unity of consciousness as the foundation of the world; rather, it steps back in order to see transcendences spring forth and it loosens the intentional threads that connect us to the world in order to make them

appear; it alone is conscious of the world because it reveals the world as strange and paradoxical . . . The world is not what I think, but what I live; I am open to the world, I unquestionably communicate with it, but I do not possess it, it is inexhaustible.

(p. 14)

What can be taken from this for the purposes of reflective practice? First and foremost, Merleau-Ponty's ideas offer a rationale for grounding reflective thought in the practitioner's lived experience, and getting away from pre-established and abstract ways of thinking about psychological problems. His notion that openness to experience, in and of itself, can start to reveal strange and paradoxical meanings, is both inspiring and unsettling. I do wonder about the rather enigmatic and absolute terms of Merleau-Ponty's argument, which could serve to intimidate rather than encourage the enthusiastic reflective practitioner. Ultimately it is impossible to entirely distinguish the real from the abstract or the symbolic, to separate fact or 'facticity' from more fictional and idealised aspects of representation. There is always a gap between experience and the language we use to describe it. In reflective practice what probably works best is a practical and gradual approach to developing members' engagement with lived experience of their practice. The aim is to encourage them to generate material that is more rather than less connected at a human and relational level, and less self-consciously processed than it might have been.

Second, Merleau-Ponty's assertion of the primacy of subjective and inter-subjective experience provides a strong rationale for ensuring that proper space is given to one member to generate material in a reflective practice session, building from this to see what the thoughts and responses of others can offer in terms of developing thinking about an issue. The clarity of thought which Merleau-Ponty brings to bear in defining a basic unit of experience as rooted in the subjective realm and then in the relationship between subject and object, underscores the value of delimiting the subjective field of interest in this way.

Experience as a psychoanalytic psychotherapist has influenced my sense of the what and the how of the Generation stage. Reflective practice and psychoanalytic supervision have in common the goal of developing self-awareness and knowledge of relational processes and particularly, unconscious aspects of these. Psychoanalytic supervision contrasts with other forms of supervision in that it looks, not just at the client and the difficulty they are bringing, but at the interactions between client and therapist, and the feelings which emerge in the relationship between them. In this type of clinical supervision this is a sustained focus; whereas in reflective practice groups with healthcare staff from a range of professional backgrounds, the aim should be to develop awareness and understanding of what might be going on in relationships with clients, particularly when this is having a clear impact on the clinical situation.

In psychoanalytic supervision you have the sense of closely observing yourself in relation to the client you are working with; whereas it is quite usual in my experience for other forms of supervision to look exclusively, or at least mostly, at the client. Intrinsic to the growth of a sense of identity as a psychoanalytic practitioner is the development of the capacity to reflect on yourself in working relationships, and to do this in an open and balanced way, combining honesty about difficulties with compassion and understanding (Casement, 1985; Ogden, 2005). Likewise, during the Generation stage of a reflective practice group, the facilitator aims to encourage a focus on the practitioner's real experience of the work and on relationships with clients and colleagues, rather than just on clients and their problems. This needs to be done with patience and sensitivity: after all, it can feel very exposing to bring the details of one's own practice before colleagues, and much easier to hide behind the difficulties of clients.

Summary

- The Generation stage involves the production of material from the lived experience of clinical practice, usually by one member for the reflective consideration of the group as a whole.
- Material should be brought to reflective practice in a way that is congruent with its aims of developing thinking about clinical dilemmas by drawing on the intellectual, human and creative resources of the group, and through the exploration of feelings and the experience of relationships on the ground.
- Members should be encouraged to bring material that is as rich and detailed as possible, with a focus on human interest and the experience of feelings and relationships in the clinical situation, and moving away from abstract technical description.
- In groups where members work closely together and share clients and colleagues, they should hold back and allow an individual colleague to generate material for themselves as an individual; the group should listen to what is brought in its specificity and avoid reducing it to something general, which everyone assumes they know about.

- Generation of material by one member of the group is followed by questions from other members so a fuller picture can develop of the situation and the people and relationships within it.
- An atmosphere of safety in the group is crucial in allowing members to bring real experiences from practice, including areas of uncertainty and confusion, although an element of risk seems to be intrinsic to the experience of opening up about real areas of uncertainty and confusion.
- Members should be encouraged to bring observations about interactions between themselves and the client, and the detail of what they said and did (even if surprised by this) rather than focusing exclusively on the client.
- There should be space to name and explore associative links, reactions on the part of the practitioners that do not seem to fit or make sense but may shed a light on something useful as thinking develops.
- Members should take it in turns to generate material for reflective practice in such a way that all members participate in doing so, but that as far as possible members can use the resources of the group when needed. The best way of doing this is for the group to organise a loose rota so someone takes responsibility for generating material each time, but members can swap with each other if it makes sense to do so.
- Creative techniques are sometimes useful in freeing up thinking during this stage; they include creative writing, visual and dramatic exercises.
- This stage draws from the phenomenological approach to philosophy, which develops conceptual thinking from foundations in the lived experience of individuals, and sees material as always rooted in a subjective or intersubjective context.

References

Bienart, H. & Clohessy, S. (2017) *Effective supervisory relationships: best evidence and practice.* Chichester, West Sussex: John Wiley & Sons Ltd.

Casement, P. (1985) *On learning from the patient.* London: Routledge.

Ladany, N., Hill, C.E., Corbett, M.M. & Nutt, E.A. (1996) Nature, extent and importance of what psychotherapy trainees do not disclose to their supervisors. *Journal of Counseling Psychology*, 43(1): 10–24.

Ladany, N., Mori, Y. & Mehr, K.W. (2013) Effective and ineffective supervision. *The Counseling Psychologist*, 41: 28–47.

Menzies Lyth, I. (1960) A case study in the functioning of social systems as a defence against anxiety: a report on a study of the nursing service of a general hospital. *Human Relations*, 13(2): 95–121.

Merleau-Ponty, M. (2012, first published 1945) *The phenomenology of perception*. London: Routledge.

Ogden, T. (2005) On psychoanalytic supervision. *International Journal of Psychoanalysis*, 86(5): 1265–1280.

7 Free Response

What is Free Response?

During the Free Response stage members are invited to share their more immediate reactions to the material brought to the group and to explore their intuitive and emotional responses to it. The aim is to reconnect with feelings and bodily sensations and to acknowledge and begin to look at spontaneous thoughts and associations, and also at opinions and snap judgements. The coordination of this activity with the next stage of More Effortful Thinking is at the core of the Intersubjective Model. The Free Response stage offers a space for the expression of curiosity and spontaneity, providing the opportunity to enrich and expand the material which has been brought from the practice setting before the group moves on to give this more deliberate consideration. In this way emotions and creative, more associative thinking can be integrated into reflections on practice, rather than sidestepped or avoided.

In my experience it is quite common to have one of these two stages without the other in a reflective practice group. However, it is most helpful to attend to them both in the course of a reflective practice session, or over two or three sessions. In the life of a group it is often necessary to focus on one or other of these stages at a particular point in time, building up the group's capacity in one of these key areas to get to a point when the two are working in tandem with each other.

It is usually helpful for the person who has generated material for the group to sit out for the Free Response and More Effortful Thinking stages. This is so that members start to work with what they have, rather than going back to their colleague with more questions; seeking further information can become a way of not sharing thoughts and feelings in response to the material, and it is useful to draw a line under information-gathering at this point. If the person who has generated material sits out it allows members at a distance from the clinical situation to focus on what they think about it, and for the group to keep members' responses distinct from those of their colleague who is more actively involved. It is also a powerful experience for the person who has generated material to watch and listen to the reactions of others, giving them space to take in alternative perspectives. This is a technique adapted from family therapy, in which there is a break in the therapy session for the family to observe the responses of a reflecting team, a small group of professionals who have been watching from behind a one-way screen (Andersen, 1987).

The rationale for the Free Response stage is fourfold. Firstly, healthcare professionals often work in services which operate in reductive and dehumanising ways for both staff and clients, and this activity gives the opportunity to reconnect with the abundant common sense, intuitive wisdom and life experience possessed by most staff. The invitation to set professional jargon to one side for a while and respond more freely to the material can be very helpful in developing the confidence of staff and rebuilding a personal relationship to work. In doing this they can learn to feel more present, and more themselves, in the clinical task. Secondly, if more automatic reactions can be observed by the group in a way that feels safe and non-blaming, some of the unhelpful and often unconscious reactions all of us have can be identified and looked at. This can lead to the prevention of mistakes and improved clinical practice. Thirdly, emotional responses to the work can start to be explored at this stage, and the process of making sense of these will often carry on in the More Effortful Thinking stage. This can be extremely beneficial to staff who are struggling with feelings they are having in response to a particular person or situation, and are confused or worried about them. It can also be helpful for clients, since emotional responses in staff can convey important information about clients' needs and ways of relating if staff have the space to acknowledge the emotional communication and to figure out its meaning. And fourthly, freer responding in human services allows staff to develop creative and unusual perspectives on problems, drawing on their resources both as individuals and as a group. To this end, it invites them to think outside of the box, bringing a range of experience to bear on the human situation presented to them.

It is worth making explicit the multifold nature of the way in which spontaneous and automatic reactions are conceptualised within the Intersubjective Model. As Daniel Kahnemann (2011) has described in his book *Thinking, Fast and Slow*, the system of thought that operates quickly and automatically in our brains does a great deal of

Table 7.1 Reasons for exploring different types of response at the Free Response stage

Variety of responses to explore	Rationale for this
More immediate responses and automatic thoughts and reactions	Put staff in touch with intuitive responses (what they know but may have forgotten they know) and enable thinking about erroneous assumptions
Emotional responses	Help staff process feelings to avoid becoming burnt out and disconnected, and allow access to an invaluable source of information about clients and the therapeutic relationship
Associative thinking – links to the material, which may be unusual or unexpected (for example, a story that comes to mind)	Help staff think 'outside the box', bringing experience from outside the field to bear on a problem shared and gaining access to unconscious processes

valuable work, applying ways of approaching problems and challenges from past situations to the present with a minimal amount of conscious effort. But it also gets things wrong, and when it comes to complex clinical situations, which are by their nature unique and unfamiliar, an over-reliance on the fast, automatic part of our brain is likely to lead to errors of judgement. Part of the problem is that the operation of what Kahnemann calls Thinking System 1 (otherwise known as thinking fast) is largely unconscious, and so it is hard for us to be aware of when and how we are using it.

Henry Marsh (2014), in his book *Do No Harm*, reflects on some of the mistakes he made during his career as a brain surgeon, using the literature on cognitive biases as a way of understanding his errors of judgement. One of his key points is that all clinicians, no matter how well-trained and vigilant they are, make such mistakes, although more often than not these are kept hidden. His work stands as a powerful argument for the need for healthcare professionals to find ways of bringing automatic ways of thinking out into the open so they can get better at detecting errors and biases. In complex, challenging situations, this type of automatic thinking will need to be replaced with more deliberate, careful consideration of a problem. Kahnemann calls this Thinking System 2 (otherwise known as thinking slow) and describes this system as more conscious than System 1 and also much harder work.

There is certainly a degree of overlap between Kahnemann's Thinking System 1 and the Free Response Stage, and a large amount of overlap between his Thinking System 2 and the More Effortful Thinking Stage. However Free Response is not the same as Thinking System 1; and More Effortful Thinking is not the same as Thinking System 2. The Free Response stage is about more than looking at automatic, reactive thinking and deciding when it should be cast inside in favour of something more considered. It involves sharing immediate responses and associations with the expectation that some of these will provide really useful leads, even if some will need to be cast aside; it also includes bringing emotional and feeling responses to the work out into the open. It is about both thought and feeling, combining a quick, associative mode with something deeper and potentially more searching.

In Kahnemann's scheme Thinking System 2 (thinking slow) comes into play when Thinking System 1 (thinking fast) is not working properly, and the latter is then replaced by the former. But within the Intersubjective Model of Reflective Practice Groups there is continuity between the Free Response and More Effortful Thinking stages, and the Free Response Stage generates material that forms the basis for deliberation in the More Effortful Thinking Stage. It is helpful for groups to think about their automatic reactions, rather than just to dismiss them, and to weave their emotional responses to the work into the way they give meaning to the situation presented to them.

I sometimes think it is easier to define the Free Response stage of reflective practice in terms of what it is not rather than what it is. This is because this stage is as much about not doing certain things as it is about doing other things. The Free Response stage involves learning to create a space for thinking that is not overly reliant on a language of clarity and certainty, or discourse that is too cognitive and abstract or that relies extensively on the pre-existing, static and sometimes rigid classification systems that operate in healthcare organisations.

In this respect facilitating reflective practice groups at the stage is partly about helping healthcare staff unlearn aspects of their professional and technical armoury, and the habitual ways they have developed of responding to clinical dilemmas and problems, at least to the extent to which they get in the way of a grounded, curious and emotionally connected approach to the work. This means that being invited to respond freely to clinical material can feel, at least at first, very unfamiliar and anxiety-provoking. Reflective practice groups in the early stages have certainly commented that the Free Response stage does not feel free at all, in the sense of being easy or straightforward.

However I have chosen to keep the name because it conveys the fact that, if a group works at unearthing this way of thinking and responding over time, it is liberating and opens up new perspectives on clinical work. Groups usually have to work at making their responses freer, and it is best not to expect things to happen too fast.

Healthcare professionals have various specialised ways of talking about clients or patients and the situations they face, which can be helpful but can also close down thinking. As an example, in the UK National Health Service there are different forms of classification that are in currency; the most dominant are the psychiatric diagnostic systems DSM-V and ICD-10, which group different types of symptoms together and allow for clinical predictions and treatment recommendations on the basis of general knowledge in the field.

These classification systems have value and utility, but if they are overused or applied in a broad-brush fashion they can drastically delimit the way in which clients are thought about and understood by healthcare staff. Most particularly they can get in the way of thinking in an open and creative way about the individual, which might be just what is needed to crack the type of problem or conundrum that colleagues bring to a reflective practice group. I have had many experiences of reflective practice groups in which staff bring a client for consideration to the group, presenting little more than a diagnosis and a couple of other details. The sense of the person in the client – their history, their family and relationships, their interests and strengths – is often missing.

There have been many criticisms over the years of the use and overuse of the language of psychiatric diagnosis in services for those presenting with psychological distress, and the way in which ideas of madness and mental illness represent sufferers as people struck down by an alien affliction rather than fellow humans who can be engaged with and understood, both as individual personalities and in their social and historical contexts (Coles, Keenan & Diamond, 2013). *The Power, Threat and Meaning Framework* offers an alternative to diagnostic systems for understanding psychological difficulties; it does not focus on symptoms, but aims to help practitioners generate meaning for individual clients in context and to get alongside them in understanding the impact of life experiences (Johnstone & Boyle, 2018).

Clinical psychologists regard psychological formulation, rather than diagnosis, as the hallmark of their professional practice, largely on the basis that formulations are fuller descriptive responses to individual clients and problems, and more readily produce ideas about the causes of a difficulty, which then inform a psychosocial intervention. However we should remind ourselves that any language that gives meaning to distress can be used in a reified way, which functions to close down new thinking, or can be applied in a fresh and open way which enables transformed perspectives. The point here is that the Free Response stage should promote direct, open engagement with clinical material, and concepts should be used in a way which aids this type of connection. It is not so much the particular language that is used, but how it is used.

There are two further tendencies of healthcare professionals which can function as obstructions to more intuitive, grounded thinking about clinical material. One is the over-reliance on abstract, higher-order thinking. This is common in clinical psychologists and psychiatrists, who are used to competing intellectually and sometimes find it hard to stop. There is nothing wrong with applying intelligence to clinical problems: we need as much of it as we can get. But in my experience practitioners can move to invoke concepts and ideas prematurely, without having explored and got up close to the material first. The other is an over-hasty adoption of an action planning mode, when practitioners start making suggestions about what to do early on in a reflective practice session, whether to recommend a treatment (based on speedy diagnostic labelling of a problem) or a referral to this or that service or professional colleague.

The ground is set for an intuitive and emotionally connected mode of response when colleagues are relatively free of the pressure to classify the problem in a static way, or to rush to demonstrate their understanding of what is going on or their knowledge of what should be done.

Illustration: a reflective practice group considers a family and is able to use the emotional responses and associations to develop a sense of the feelings and perspective of different family members

I was co-facilitating a reflective practice group of trainee clinical psychologists. The group had been meeting once a month for a little over a year.

We started by reminding ourselves about the previous seminar. Laura had told us about a client who she felt drawn to; this was someone who she could well imagine making friends with if she had not been her therapist. She did not know if she had been over-friendly with her client, and it had also been hard to say goodbye. It was funny to think that she would never see her again. Sharing a personal reaction in this way enabled others in the group to talk about similar feelings, and we had a good discussion about how endings feel from the practitioner's point of view.

Ben then said he had a case he wanted to talk about. The theme of a client to whom one feels strongly connected carried over from one seminar to the next, although we did not notice this at the time. Ben told us about a family he had just started seeing in a Family Therapy Clinic. The family consisted of a twelve-year-old boy, Jonathan, his father, Alex, and his stepmother, Holly. Jonathan had been known to Child and Adolescent Services for some years. His parents had split up when he was little, and he had lived with his mother and his younger brother until a couple of years before, when he was removed from his mother's care because of concerns about his safety. He did not have any contact with his mother, but his father did facilitate contact with his brother once a week.

The family was seeking help because of Jonathan's extreme fits of temper at home and school. He had recently broken something that was particularly precious to Holly. Ben told us that when the family arrived it was Holly who spoke; she seemed highly anxious and 'a bit much'. Jonathan was a bright boy and seemed to take charge of things, telling Ben about his parents in a rather grown-up way. Alex, his father, was quite withdrawn and difficult to get a sense of.

After Ben had described the family and the set-up in the family therapy clinic, I asked him what he wanted to get out of the seminar. He said he had thought it would be interesting to bring a family to reflective practice and not an individual. He wondered how to think about a whole family rather than just one person. Ben then tentatively said something about how much he liked Jonathan: he seemed so smart and appealing. It seemed Ben had started to feel curious about how he felt about Jonathan. We asked Ben to withdraw – to sit outside the circle – and let the rest of us get on with some thinking on his behalf.

I invited the group to share reactions. Family material is usually comparatively easy to relate to; a couple of members spoke about what a bright spark Jonathan was, and began to think about what a difficult time he had had and how little information we had about his early life and his 'other family', meaning his mother and his brother. Jane then said she really felt for Jonathan; she was angry on his behalf and thought the grown-ups in his life had repeatedly let him down. No wonder he felt he had to take charge of things and lost his temper. She went a step further and told us she was seething: she felt furious when she thought about his situation.

In contrast my thoughts were with Holly, Ben's step-mother, and it was tempting to react to Jane by putting Holly's case. But I felt I should validate Jane's emotional response before anything else, and also hold to the boundaries of the facilitator's role. When people start opening up about feelings this can be hard to do. I asked Jane to tell us more and this led to thoughts in the group about what Jonathan had gone through, and an increased understanding of why he might be behaving in a commanding and superior way. Then Katy said she had a different reaction to Jonathan; she thought he was a 'manipulative little shit'! There was laughter at this point, and a sense of release. There was also an air of challenge, and Katy and Jane looked at each other with humour and a certain recognition of their different alignments. The discussion opened up and some people in the group spoke about how difficult things must be for Holly, and how hard she was trying – perhaps too hard – to stay positive and to be forgiving. Thoughts then moved onto Alex, and how it was difficult to connect with him and to have a sense of what he was going through. It was easy to forget that he had lived with Jonathan's mother for some years and had had four children with her; he was at least partly responsible for what had gone wrong in the family.

My co-facilitator summarised where we had got to, noticing the different, strong reactions different people had to the various family members. We wanted the group to take an interest in these alignments as they moved towards trying to make sense of what was going on in the family: the More Effortful Thinking stage. I asked the group about their thoughts about Alex and why it was hard to connect with him, as I wanted to widen the discussion and avoid people taking either Holly or Jonathan's side. There were some critical comments about Alex, and Anna then thought about how Alex might 'not be able to go there' in terms of feeling responsible for what had gone wrong and, therefore, was not able to engage emotionally with Jonathan in the way Holly could. There was an interesting discussion of how Alex's vulnerability and his difficulty in processing what had happened really needed to be recognised, partly because of the impact it was having on Holly and Jonathan. In the later stages of the seminar we seemed to be able to sympathise with all three family members, and to think in a more fluid way about what they were struggling with on an individual and family level. It was as if they had become three- rather than two-dimensional people in our minds.

Critical issues from practice

In this section I will describe three key issues in the facilitation of free responses to clinical material in reflective practice groups, with suggestions for how to address them. These are: the tendency for healthcare staff to close down thinking rather than open it up, speaking in a specialist way about what is going on or moving prematurely into an action-oriented mode; the very normal struggle practitioners experience in being invited to share emotions and personal associations to material in a work setting, and how to offer a form of facilitation that makes this feels both safe and productive; and the risk inherent in entering a more explorative mode of people feeling too exposed and vulnerable, either because of something they have themselves shared with the group or because of something someone else has said. It is only possible to move into the Free Response stage when people feel safe enough to open up and take risks, and safety is something that has to be carefully and patiently developed in a group setting in most modern healthcare organisations.

When colleagues start a new job or visit an unfamiliar service they often observe that healthcare staff use a bewildering array of technical terms and jargon, and particularly acronyms, in order to talk about clients and the teams and services with which they liaise. When you have worked in one of these services for a while it is easy to become deaf to the extent to which jargon is used. This is useful because it provides professionals with a convenient shorthand, but it contains within it assumptions about what we are doing and why, which it can be useful to examine or to get away from altogether.

In his book *The Reflective Practitioner* Donald Schon (1983) considers the function of the highly technical language of professional expertise in our modern, post-Enlightenment. He suggests that it partly operates to convey power and status, both within and between professional groups. He gives amusing and informative accounts of the way in which professional bodies have sought to claim technological or scientific status and to distance themselves from what is thought, wrongly or rightly, to be unscientific – or worse mystical. This makes sense of the way in which outsiders can find it difficult, if not impossible, to understand what is being spoken about; and I am afraid clients or patients often feel like outsiders when faced with the bewildering array of technical terms and service acronyms used by healthcare professionals.

Schon thought that technical language, if used to the exclusion of other forms of thought and expression about many types of work, can get in the way of practitioners drawing on their intuitive wisdom and common sense. It can also close down thinking about how a problem is approached, since technical discourse tends to fit together particular types of problems with particular types of pre-defined solutions, when it might be more helpful to ask questions about how best to define both the problem and the outcome. Schon calls this reframing the problem, and he presents it as a core task of reflective practice.

It sometimes happens that one is asked to facilitate a group of healthcare practitioners who find it comparatively easy to talk in more intuitive, immediate and human terms about the work. But it is more usual for the facilitator to need to find ways of nudging the group towards responding in a freer way to clinical material, and helping them give up some of the technical language and professional armoury with which they are familiar, certainly in healthcare services in the UK National Health Service where I work. Initially, I invite group members to respond in a more ordinary and emotionally connected way to the material by saying something like this: 'We've just heard about X, and I guess we're beginning to build a picture of them in our minds. What do you see?' I find that this shift to the visual encourages people to explore the way they have started to represent the people they have heard about. Later on, I might ask: 'What are your reactions to what we have heard?' And: 'What are your feelings?'

Sometimes the clinical material will have obviously had an emotional impact on the group, and it seems right to ask how people have been affected from the off. But asking this question at the start can intimidate practitioners and make them feel put on the spot. In trying to get things going at this stage, I have learnt to avoid the question 'What are your thoughts?' because this gets interpreted as a request for higher-order thinking about the case. I have also learnt that I sometimes need to persist in helping groups make the transition to this stage, repeating the invitation to focus on the immediate and the intuitive, and sometimes making an observation when a group is finding this particularly difficult.

I routinely model reacting to the material presented, sharing an emotional response or an association, particularly at the beginning stage of the group. There is obviously a risk in doing this that the group gets taken up with my reaction rather than looking at their own responses, or becomes dependent on me taking a lead in this way. Such sharing on the part of the facilitator should be undertaken to model a more open and less self-conscious approach, and the facilitator should try to step back into their role fairly quickly. So I try to keep what I say pretty minimal, and do not share a complicated or heightened reaction.

Groups can sometimes be quite inhibited about opening up as the result of anxiety about personal exposure and vulnerability in a work setting. It is helpful to regard this as normal and not to feel too frustrated and disappointed about the hard work necessary to get going with the Free Response stage. I have found that small gains during this stage yield big results. By this I mean that a subtle shift in the spontaneity and emotional feel of clinical discussion can have a transformative effect on the way the group understands and gives meaning to the clinical task. The job of the facilitator is to help the group feel safe enough to begin to explore feelings and reactions more intuitively. The main way of achieving this is to bring thinking back to the clinical task, usually during the More Effortful Thinking stage, thus allaying anxiety that reflective practice is therapy by stealth. During the Free Response stage one can begin to make sense of feelings in this way, inviting members to participate widely to normalise feeling responses to the work and make sure an individual does not feel isolated in having expressed an emotion. One can also start to make links which suggest that practitioners' feelings have something to tell us about what is going on inside an individual client and in their relationships with others with questions like: 'Do you think that X feels that way too?' Or: 'Do you think other people feel that way towards X?'

The Free Response stage is an invitation to play, to explore feelings and associations without too much attention being given to what they mean, at least initially. As we know from attachment theory, exploration and play are enabled by a sense of emotional security. The small toddler who is safe and securely rooted in their attachment to a caregiver will be more able to play and to investigate what is going on out in the world. It is no different in reflective practice groups, in which it seems that the capacity of the group to explore thoughts and feelings with creativity and freedom is contingent on an atmosphere of safety and trust.

Mark Loveder (2017) carried out a grounded theory study on what trainee clinical psychologists found useful about reflective practice groups from the point of view of practice. I supervised his research, which consisted of a careful analysis of interviews with trainee clinical psychologists attending a three-year reflective practice group, co-facilitated by two clinical colleagues. The group was considered, overall, to be constructive and helpful. Loveder found that group members were continually monitoring how safe it felt to share experiences from practice in an open and honest way, and saw the group as useful to their clinical work when they felt able to do this. Group members paid close attention to the reactions of others when a colleague made what was described as a more personal disclosure, and calibrated their own contributions in response to what they observed. Trust and safety were ongoing and important aspects of the experience for the group: they were not optional extras, but had a direct effect on the ability of members to make real use of the resource. This suggests the importance of facilitators attending closely to the sense of safety and trust in a reflective practice group, perhaps particularly at the Free Response stage. They should ask about this at review points and take notice of interactions which increase or decrease the trust group members have in each other to respond in a thoughtful, positive and respectful way.

Techniques

The Free Response stage is intended to provide an open space for staff to explore reactions, so the use of specific procedures is kept fairly minimal because they tend to prescribe and delimit responses. However I do normally rely on what I think of as the 'sitting out technique', which is adapted from the use of the reflecting team in therapeutic work with families (Andersen, 1987). I ask the presenter to sit outside the circle to observe their colleagues responding to what they have said, just as a family coming for therapy is invited to watch and listen to the reflecting team who have been observing their interactions from behind a one-way screen. I ask them to sit out during the Free Response and More Effortful Thinking stages. This is because I have found that if they remain part of discussions it is considerably more difficult for the group to do something with the material it has got. Instead members keep referring to the authority of the colleague who knows the people involved, or the presenting colleague interjects with comments or corrections, which can get in the way of the

Table 7.2 Advice regarding critical issues at the Free Response stage

Critical issue	Summary of advice for the facilitator
Tendency to wrap up thinking using professional jargon or move prematurely into action planning	Invite members to draw on their ordinary, human ways of responding to the situation presented
Difficulty in opening up with regard to more immediate responses and emotional reactions to the work	Invite members to look at feelings and associations; use feeling words and model emotional responses in the early stages of group
The risk inherent in sharing responses more freely and openly than staff are used to	Give space to processing responses in terms of what they can tell us about the clinical task; be sensitive to how safe the group feels at different points in time and revisit contract if necessary

development of new lines of thought. In addition if the person who has shared something from practice sits out, they are more able to simply listen to and take in the thoughts and responses of others, which is very useful for them.

There are also some techniques I routinely use with staff who are finding it difficult to get going at this stage. Early on in the life of a reflective practice group it is often helpful to model responding with emotion and curiosity to the material presented. So I will talk, for example, about feeling warmly towards a client or irritated, or I will let the group know that I cannot bring someone to mind or am intrigued by some aspect of the case. There are two provisos here. As a facilitator I filter my reactions a little, with the aim of modelling a free response without imposing myself too much. If I was troubled by my reaction, I would not immediately let the group know about it. Also as group members become more able to use the space I will take a back seat, keeping the focus on group members' reactions rather than my own.

Techniques which encourage group members to react to material associatively, as if it were a story in a book or a film, thinking of the people as characters and the events as a plot or unfolding narrative, can be very freeing. I have written about these more fully in the chapter on Generation, alongside visual and dramatic approaches to opening up thinking about clinical material. They seem to get the creative juices going and to reduce the sense of anxious responsibility staff often feel in relation to the real seriousness of their work. They also enable a focus on the way in which group members represent clinical material to themselves, on how they begin to process and take it in, which is an important and often neglected determinant of the staff-patient relationship.

The move away from professional language to the language of image, story and feeling can help staff name an elusive aspect to their experience; and, sometimes, going outside the box of normal professional terms of reference can be of direct benefit to thinking about a case. As an example, I was in a group in which we were discussing a young boy who had experienced a great deal of trauma and struck us as someone with considerable strengths as well as areas of difficulty. There was something about this boy which was hard to describe. He was defended and wary as a result of all he had suffered, but he had such a strong and unique character as well; he had a great deal of integrity, and there was something very individual about his sense of humour and way of looking at the world. I had recently read the novel by J.M Coetzee (1983), *The Life and Times of Michael K*. It is set in

South Africa in the 1970s during a fictional civil war. It describes the experience of a young black man with a hare lip who makes a journey with his sick mother to the place of her birth. He is looked down upon and oppressed throughout, but what comes across powerfully in the narrative is a personal form of resistance to oppression, a way in which Michael K exerts himself through the tenacity of his actions and reactions. This notion of resistance, in its political sense, came to mind in connection with the boy we were talking about in the group. It seemed more helpful than the traditional concept of defence as a means of understanding the way in which he had managed to protect, and indeed discover, the force of his personality in the face of such trauma and hardship.

Key influences

Donald Schon's seminal book, *The Reflective Practitioner*, is a powerful argument for the legitimacy and authority of a particular type of reflective thinking in professional life. Schon argues for the value of reflective practice as a corrective to our post-Enlightenment preoccupation with scientific and technical knowledge, and its association with professionalism. He gives examples of the ways in which various professional bodies have striven to gain status by claiming scientific credibility and distancing themselves from what is represented as non-scientific, and even as mystical, forms of knowing and doing. His book shows us what is lost by this reaction against pre-Enlightenment thought, and in particular, the way it links the non-rational – or the not yet rationally understood – with religiosity and the notion of blind belief.

Schon's view is that an exclusive focus on technological expertise, with standardised methods and predefined outcomes, risks cutting practitioners off from their curiosity about the new and the unknown, and from their intuitive wisdom and practical know-how. The emphasis all the time on specialist expertise – on superior knowledge gained through the pursuit of expensive training and qualifications – can make staff feel immensely deskilled. The Free Response stage has, therefore, partly been developed to help practitioners reconnect with their ordinary, human responses to the valuable and interesting work they do. It bears Schon's imprint, with its aim of groundedness in the real, lived experience of work in human services and the development of confidence in the belief that, over time, unearthing these responses and exploring their meaning will be validating and useful for practitioners.

The Free Response stage of the Intersubjective Model of group reflective practice places an emphasis on looking at the feelings evoked in practitioners by their work, and has been influenced by my training and experience as a psychoanalytic psychotherapist in the use of countertransference responses. What this means is that the model places at its centre the task of helping staff gain an awareness of their emotional reactions to clinical situations, and of giving these meaning in the clinical context. This is justified by the now substantial empirical evidence that developing an understanding of countertransference responses, and managing them effectively, is associated across therapeutic modalities with successful therapeutic relationships and good outcomes (Norcross, 2011).

Freud and Klein both regarded the countertransference, by which I mean the feelings evoked in the therapist in response to the client, as an unwelcome obstruction to therapeutic work and something to be put to one side and dealt with through personal therapy. Paula Heimann's seminal paper of 1950 marked a turning point in psychoanalytic thinking about the countertransference (Heimann, 1950). In it she describes a fear of emotion in her psychoanalytic colleagues, which she regards as off-putting to patients, and she puts forward the view that feelings in the clinical situation can be of real and immense clinical utility. Psychoanalytic practitioners today are trained to attend closely to their feeling states when they are with patients; they learn about the power of unconscious communication in the therapeutic relationship, and the value of remaining curious and thoughtful in the face of strong and sometimes perplexing emotions in clinical encounters.

Patrick Casement writes in an articulate way about what he calls 'communication by impact' between patient and therapist (Casement, 1985). He draws on the work of Donald Winnicott and others in his view of the clinical value of enactments, when the therapist is struggling with what is going on in the transference-countertransference relationship and does something unhelpful as a result. Such enactments, certainly on a small scale, are inevitable, and are also very helpful if they can be learned from. As a reflective practitioner, I have been influenced by a psychoanalytic tradition which tries not to be afraid of 'mistakes', of aspects of practice which might initially look messy or confused or even 'wrong', regarding them instead as an inevitable part of working in an engaged way with human problems and distress. The Intersubjective Model aims to create a safe environment so staff can look honestly and thoughtfully at the human work they do, and so they feel able to acknowledge and think about emotional responses rather than pretending they do not exist. Under-lying this aspect of the model is the rationale that, if these responses can be thought about rather than brushed under the carpet, larger-scale enactments and serious mistakes can be avoided.

I have had a longstanding interest in the power of the unconscious mind and the creativity inherent in good therapeutic work. In this, I have been influenced by psychoanalytic writers such as Donald Win-nicott, and more recently Thomas Ogden and Margot Waddell, who in their clinical papers have described the development of a creative, playful space to free up thinking and explore unconscious commu-nication (Ogden, 2001; Winnicott, 1971; Waddell, 2010). What I have taken from these authors is a serious commitment to the value of play in clinical work, by which I mean the importance of having a space where the different or unusual or surprising can be thought about. Play, in other words, is a serious business – particularly when it comes to unearthing unconscious content. As an example, Margot Waddell describes the creative process of a therapy session in detail to demon-strate how misleading preconceived ideas about human situations can be; she shows how high-quality clinical work involves making careful use of associations to move with the patient beyond a surface narrative to discover a deeper and more complicated truth.

It is to be expected that some individuals and groups will be more responsive than others to the invitation to explore links and use the imagination in this way. The Free Response stage exists as a space to develop, over time, curiosity and associative thinking, offering an opportunity for groups to make their own creative links – if and when they are ready to do so.

For some years now, colleagues and I have organised an observational task for trainee clinical psychologists on the Leicester course, which is informed by the psychodynamic observational method. We have drawn particularly on the work of R.D. Hinshelwood and Wilhelm Skogstad in describing an observational method designed to develop trainee doctors' understanding of healthcare culture (Hinshelwood & Skogstad, 2000). This activity has involved facilitating small groups whose aim is to make sense of raw observational material, and from it I have learnt a great deal about the nature of unconscious communication in study groups. As in the Illustration for this chapter, I have been struck by the way in which group members will pick up on the submerged or hidden aspects of their colleague's presentation, responding in a different way to the material or wondering about what is suggested in it but not made explicit. A common example of this is when an observer presents the patients in a ward setting sympathetically and the staff less so, identifying initially with one group and not with another. It often then happens that those listening begin to wonder about the characters that are more sketchily and less empathically presented, helping the observer open out their understanding of a complex network of relationships.

Hinshelwood and Skogstad make the point that the observer will have picked up on things which they are not aware of, and what the group members are often doing is filling in these blind spots. There is a risk that this can make the observer feel inept or stupid, and it is helpful to enable the group to show their colleague that they know and feel more than they are consciously aware of knowing and feeling. As Hinshelwood and Skogstad write:

> It is important for the seminar group to acknowledge the observer's intuition, and to help them become aware of what they have picked up instinctively but are perhaps not aware of – at least not at first. Likewise, it is useful for the facilitator to convey the sense that the creation of a fuller picture of what might be going on in the clinical situation is seen as normal and natural, so the presenter is not made to feel inadequate for having initially shared what will inevitably be a partial and selective account.
>
> (p. 23)

Summary

- During the Free Response stage, practitioners are invited to connect with their more immediate and intuitive reactions to the material presented, to begin to acknowledge and explore emotional responses, and to think 'outside the box', sharing associations and creative links.
- Freeing up responses in this way can help groups make use of the intuitive wisdom of the group, which an over-emphasis on the language of technical expertise can make it hard to access; it can allow practitioners to identify and modify automatic reactions which are unhelpful or counter-therapeutic; it can enable exploration of feelings engendered by the work, which can be supportive to staff and help them better understand their clients; and it can open up new and valuable perspectives on clinical problems.
- It is useful to ask the person who has generated material for the group to sit out during the Free Response and More Effortful Thinking stages so they can benefit from listening to the thoughts of others, and to enable the rest of the group to do something with the material provided rather than referring to their colleague for more information.

Table 7.3 Key influences on the Free Response stage

Influential idea and author(s)	Nature of influence on Free Response Stage
Donald Schon's argument that non-standardised, intuitive knowledge has legitimacy and authority alongside technological and scientific knowledge and expertise	Open and human nature of the inquiry into members' responses, which can be immediate thoughts, emotional responses or associations, going 'outside the box' to experiences which do not initially seem relevant
Psychoanalytic theory of the counter-transference (Paula Heimann and Patrick Casement) and the ideas that a) feeling responses in therapeutic work have a lot to tell us about what is going on; and b) small mistakes are common and staff and patients suffer if they are kept hidden	Aim of creating a safe environment in which practice can be explored honestly and openly and staff feel able to look at emotional responses to work, confident that these will be brought back to the clinical situation
Literature on the creative power of the unconscious (Thomas Ogden and Margot Waddell) and the way in which creative/associative thinking can connect us to unconscious processes	Inquiry into creative links and associations, with particular attention to thoughts and ideas that may initially seem off-limits
Hinshelwood's description of the role of the supervision group in digesting observational material	Value of exploring different responses of group members to the same material; use of group in helping observer see what they have intuited but not been consciously aware of

- Responding in a freer way can feel, paradoxically, very difficult, particularly early on in the life of a group, because it involves giving up habitual ways of responding.
- These familiar responses, which can get in the way of a Free Response, include the following: an over-reliance on technical jargon and specialist language in talking about clinical work, using this in a reified way which narrows thinking possibilities; an over-use of conceptual or abstract ways of thinking which get in the way of a more spontaneous and grounded approach; and a pressure to instruct, whereby members start to make suggestions about what to do before there has been any explorative thinking about what might be going on.
- Facilitators should be willing to work patiently over time in helping groups become less reliant on these habitual reactions and in

encouraging them to share different sorts of responses to clinical material.

• It is usual for groups to find it hard, at least initially, to share emotional reactions to the work, perhaps feeling that this is wrong or unprofessional; facilitators will need to give a sense of purpose to this activity, helping the group process responses in terms of what they have to say about the clinical task, as well as attending closely to issues of safety and trust in the group.

• Creative methods sometimes help group members open up their thinking at this stage; they include creative writing and visual and dramatic exercises.

References

Andersen, T. (1987) The reflecting team: dialogue and meta-dialogue in clinical work. *Family Process*, 26: 415–428.

Casement, P. (1985) *On learning from the patient*. London: Routledge.

Coetzee, J.M. (1983) *The life and times of Michael K*. London: Penguin Books.

Coles, S., Keenan, S. & Diamond, B. (Eds.) (2013) *Madness contested: power and practice*. Monmouth: PCCS Books.

Heimann, P. (1950) On counter-transference. *International Journal of Psycho-Analysis*, 31: 81–84.

Hinshelwood, R.D. & Skogstad, W. (2000) The method of observing organisations. In Hinshelwood, R.D. & Skogstad, W. (Eds.) *Observing organisations: anxiety, defence and culture in healthcare*. London: Routledge.

Johnstone, L. & Boyle, M. with Cromby, J., Dillon, J., Harper, D., Kinderman, P., Longden, E., Pilgrim, D. & Read, J. (2018) *The power threat meaning framework: towards the identification of patterns in emotional distress, unusual experiences and troubled or troubling behaviour, as an alternative to functional psychiatric diagnosis*. Leicester: The British Psychological Society.

Kahnemann, D. (2011) *Thinking, fast and slow*. London: Penguin Books.

Loveder, M. (2017) *Does reflective practice impact upon clinical outcomes and if so, how? A grounded theory study of how trainee clinical psychologists experience the effect of a reflective practice group on their clinical work*. Unpublished Dissertation; University of Leicester.

Marsh, H. (2014) *Do no harm: stories of life, death and brain surgery*. London: Wiedenfield & Nicolson.

Norcross, J.C. (Ed.) (2011) *Psychotherapy relationships that work: evidence-based responsiveness* (2nd ed.). Oxford: Oxford University Press.

Ogden, T.H. (2001) *Conversations at the frontier of dreaming*. London: Karnac Books.

Schon, D.A. (1983) *The reflective practitioner: how professionals think in action*. Farnham, Surrey: Ashgate Books Ltd.

Waddell, M. (2010) 'From resemblance to identity': the internal narrative of a fifty-minute hour. In Mawson, C. (Ed.) *Bion today: new library of psychoanalysis.* New York: Routledge.

Winnicott, D.W. (1971) *Playing and reality.* London: Tavistock Publications Ltd.

8 More Effortful Thinking

What Is More Effortful Thinking?

More Effortful Thinking is the stage when the group develops an understanding of the issue before it, bringing together the material generated from practice and the responses and associations which have been explored so far. It is the stage at which members of the group are invited to stand back, having learnt about what is going on and considered initial reactions and ideas, and ask the question as to what might really be going on; or, if this seems too definite and too narrow, what alternatives are there for understanding what is happening? This stage involves perspective-taking, the integration of different viewpoints and the bringing together of theory or abstract understanding with the stuff of lived experience. It is hard work thinking in this way, and it can be satisfying and frustrating by turns. So it is useful to have realistic expectations about the amount of this type of activity that a group can do together on any one occasion. For this reason I tend to ask myself whether a group has shifted into this mode during a meeting, and feel pleased if concentrated thinking has been sustained for even a brief period, rather than aiming for it to form the bulk of the group's activity.

More Effortful Thinking, together with the Generation and Free Response stages, is at the heart of the Intersubjective Model. Generation involves one member sharing their lived experience of practice with the group in as full a way as possible; Free Response is about helping the group open up in acknowledging emotions in response to the work, and in exploring new and perhaps unexpected associations; and More Effortful Thinking is about bringing together and processing these two stages to achieve a measure of coherence and closure.

The explicit consideration of psychological ideas, or concepts from another healthcare discipline, are likely to contribute to the discussion at this point. For psychologists, for example, a formulation of the issue which draws on psychological theory will form a definite part of reflective practice. But it is not psychological formulation per se, or the use of a particular set of ideas, which constitutes this stage within the Intersubjective Model. Instead this stage is about thinking in a way that is deliberate and non-reactive, and the choice of tools it uses – be they from the discipline of psychology, nursing, medicine, sociology or a different subject area altogether – should be determined by whether or not they help make sense of what is going on. It is defined more by its underlying aim of transforming understanding of an issue, than by the use of a particular kind of approach.

It may be that what a group finds most useful at this point is the application of an existing theory or therapeutic model. Indeed this is likely to be the case much of the time because there are lots of well-developed theories around. But there should also be room at this stage for something more playful and explorative to occur, whereby an experience can be linked to a concept that is not fully formed, or an idea from outside the regular professional discipline of the members of the group. Examples of this are when members bring personal experience to bear on a professional situation, drawing on their intuitive knowledge and life experience, or an idea from a TV programme or film they have seen or a book they have read. More effortful thinking emerges from the need to think about something afresh or to apply established ideas in a new context. It is, therefore, in its essence, creative.

Thinking outside the box in this way can be a helpful way of developing an understanding of a challenging or complex issue. It can be achieved by bringing together ideas in an innovative or unusual way, or by what Donald Schon (1984) calls reframing the problem. This is when a question is approached using a different perspective from the one applied in first bringing it before the group for consideration. So for example, the frame shifts from one in which there is an individual client who staff are finding difficult, to a systemic frame, which includes staff with organisational pressures on them who are, therefore, finding it hard to respond sympathetically to an individual client; or the frame shifts from one in which a member of staff feels – often with a lot of discomfort – that their negative response to an inter-personal situation reveals something unprofessional about them, to one in which the response can be seen to result from previously unexplored aspects of the relationship with the client and pressures exerted by the service context.

In his influential book *Thinking, Fast and Slow* Daniel Kahneman describes two types of thinking system which he calls Systems 1 and 2. System 1 Thinking is fast, automatic and often unconscious. System 2 Thinking is slow, deliberate and takes effort. More effortful thinking in the Intersubjective Model is to some extent the same as the sort of conscious mental activity which Kahneman defines as System 2 Thinking, which is brought into play when the more automatic and spontaneous approaches that characterise System 1 Thinking are not working.

Kahneman's presents Systems 1 and 2 Thinking as rather separate and disconnected, and in many of his examples, people do best when they cast their intuitive reactions aside and think knotty problems through deliberately. According to Kahneman when System 1 Thinking does not work, you can then choose whether or not to make the effort to think harder, drawing on System 2 Thinking. He describes an either/or type situation, rather than a both/and. But the relationship in the Intersubjective Model between the reactive and the more deliberate modes of thinking is a different one from Kahneman's. In the best-case scenario, the More Effortful Thinking stage involves working through emotional reactions or immediate thoughts so that they can be better understood when the practitioner is next in the clinical situation. It is often integrative work that groups do at this stage, involving making sense of associations, feelings and automatic reactions, processing them and getting to a new understanding that way.

This stage aims to take account of quicker and more intuitive feelings and reactions to material from practice rather than setting them aside, based on an acknowledgement of the wisdom they contain, particularly in the area of unconscious communication. So for example, reactions to the material, such as an emotional response of irritation or despair or excitement, are seen as having the potential to reveal something important about the issue being presented if they can be acknowledged and processed. The aim of this stage is to move beyond the reactive mode towards a more fully formed and considered sense of things. For this reason, More Effortful Thinking is something the group builds up to, coming to it via the stages in which, firstly, something from practice is shared and, secondly, group members air responses to the practice material in as free a way as possible.

I do think the success of this thinking stage is largely down to the extent to which group members have already engaged with the issue in a real, rather than an abstract or a more superficial, way; and the extent to which they have as individuals allowed their imagination to flow and be open to the pattern and shape of identificatory processes in the group. The latter is the way in which group members pick up on different aspects of what is presented, connecting to the material in a variety of ways as individuals. If, for example, a colleague generates a description of a family and the individuals within it, other group members will find themselves focusing on, or even siding with, one individual or another. It is fascinating to see how, in allowing space for these different partialities, these different lines of empathy, a fuller, more three-dimensional picture of the situation emerges.

Since More Effortful Thinking often involves asking the question as to what might be going on in a situation which is complicated or confusing, practitioners can become intimidated by the task, partly out of the sense that they need to find a full answer or solution. Sometimes it is possible to do this, but it is helpful to accept that this type of thinking is often provisional and incomplete, constrained by the situation and the needs of the presenting practitioner. The group should try to do the best it can with what has been placed in front of it, aiming for meaning rather than truth, certainty or completeness. Indeed if a group tries to be too formulaic or systematic in the way it applies conceptual thinking to practice, the potential to generate meaning in a more lively and creative way can be lost.

Neville Symington (1986), in his book *The Analytic Experience: Lectures from the Tavistock*, writes that the truth which psycho-analytic work aims to uncover is in the end often a simple one. I think the same can be said of the work of a reflective practice group. The value of such a truth is, firstly, in the extent to which it conveys meaning rather than in how clever or complicated it is, and secondly, in its capacity to generate further meaning and bring about an internal shift in the way something is thought about and experienced and its potential to then bring about an external change in relationships. What is most relevant during the More Effortful Thinking stage is the transformative value of the work of the group and the extent to which it can generate knowledge that can be made use of, rather than knowledge for its own sake. Less is often more when it comes to such knowledge.

This stage can be both creative and satisfying, the point at which the group, having generated material and explored a range of ideas and possibilities, gathers its thinking together and brings some sort of order to the situation. If the group is working well it will draw on the resources of members to carry this out, and the combined knowledge and experience of the group will be in operation. This stage can also be frustrating, involving a sense of not really being able to attain understanding, or not in the complete and unified way which we might wish for. It can also be difficult to integrate the viewpoints of different group members. But better a half-idea or a fragmented understanding that feels right, than something impressive and ordered that is imposed or spun out of nowhere. After all, it is always possible to revisit ideas over time and to develop understanding in an organic way as discussions progress.

This stage is in some measure usually hard and even painful work, and like all work it involves discipline. It can necessitate the relinquishment of cherished and familiar ways of looking at things, requiring practitioners to move beyond immediate responses to the situation, which can be compelling and preoccupying; it also, sometimes, asks that they face up to areas of doubt and uncertainty in their work. There is a tendency for healthcare professionals, who are mostly highly trained and strongly motivated, to expect too much of themselves when it comes to the intellectual activity of reflective practice. More Effortful Thinking is not a straightforward or easy thing to do or to keep up for any length of time; and it is helpful if facilitators take the view that it is a real achievement when a group works together in thinking deeply and creatively in this way, rather than assuming that this will happen from the off. On the other hand, if a group is meeting regularly and this type of thinking is not happening at all, or there is too little of it, members are likely to feel, at best, frustrated and, at worst, unsettled or disturbed by listening to complex and overwhelming material without finding a way to frame and contain it.

In my experience, groups can struggle to enter this stage because it is hard work and can also be exposing. It is sometimes much more appealing to exchange abstract or preliminary ideas about a problem, or to keep asking for more information about a complex and fascinating case – as if the answer lies in the unearthing of more facts – than to wrestle in an honest way with what one thinks and feels in response to a matter. What this requires, apart from anything else, is that the group lay aside a good deal of competitive anxiety in order to look together at any individual's necessarily partial and incomplete understanding of a problem, and to discover, hopefully in an atmosphere of respect, variations, and sometimes real differences, of approach.

This sounds like a simple thing to do, but in my experience it is often quite a challenge for individuals in a group to accept that they can in any real sense learn from each other. This is because, in order to do so, one needs to stop seeing others as people to impress or perform in front of, and to have enough confidence in one's own point of view not be threatened by listening to a different or opposing perspective.

Critical issues

One of the most common tendencies is for reflective practice groups to respond to the presentation of clinical material by quickly moving into an intellectual or abstract mode, offering explanations on the basis of scarce information and suggesting actions on the basis of premature understanding. In this type of situation one is met by lots of explanatory ideas or half-ideas about what is going on, without the group having a sense of what the situation is in the first place – and without this having been explored and thought about in any depth. Sometimes the ideas take the form of diagnostic labels, and the question here is whether these are being applied in a way which communicates something useful about the problem and how it is seen, or in a way which defines matters too simply and fast. The group can feel on these occasions as if there is nothing more to think or say, and as if things have already been wrapped up.

Premature meaning-making is usually the result of anxiety about not knowing what is going on, making it difficult for group members to tolerate feeling uncertain or confused, or simply having to wait to make sense of things. This can be exacerbated by the group situation and the sense members can have, particularly in the early stages, of being judged by their peers and having to perform in front of each other. In this mode, members seem keen to reassert what they already know, either as individuals or as a group, and the opportunities for new learning are constrained. In addition the atmosphere can become unhelpfully competitive, and the person presenting can feel as if they have had other people's views and opinions imposed upon them, often in quite an overwhelming way, rather than having their experience attended to properly.

Equally common is for groups to focus more on emotional responses to the work situation, getting bogged down by anxieties and frustrations, and not to manage to make the shift into a mode which offers some distance and perspective. It is as if what starts as a helpful debrief gets stuck at this stage. The group ends up in a collapsed and rather depressed state, weighed down and inactive; and the feelings provoked by what is going on seem to take over, leaving people demoralised and stuck.

There is a view that the main aim of reflective practice is the off-loading of feelings that result from clinical work, and colleagues often get asked to facilitate groups with this in mind. I do think it is important that groups move beyond the expression of reactions and spontaneous responses to do something with what is brought, either in terms of processing feelings or developing an understanding of what is going on, so that staff feel bolstered in their capacity for work. This shift from a reactive, intuitive mode to a thoughtful and more deliberate one is at the heart of the Intersubjective Model. Reactions and intuitions are seen as an important source of clinical information, aiding understanding and empathic relating with clients if properly understood; on the other hand, thoughtful processing of these by the group should, over time, encourage staff to open up to each other, confident that something useful will be gained.

Another familiar issue relates to the question as to how open or closed a group is in its thinking. It is common for a reflective practice group to feel pressure to resolve the dilemma put before it. Of course it is satisfying when this happens, but it is not productive for meaning to be too forced. The effect can be one in which some good links between theory and practice are sacrificed to an overly formulaic approach to the problem; or in which some members of the group express what seems like a complete understanding of what is going on, but other members feel confused and excluded from this knowledge. One of the main aims of the group is to build staff's confidence in their ability to use themselves as a resource, outside the group as well as in. This can be undermined if there is too much pressure to reach a complete solution each time the group meets.

Alternatively the group can be messy and chaotic in its thinking, something that is more likely to happen when group members have different approaches in the way they understand problems. So for example, there are groups in which there is a range of ideas offered to give meaning to the situation, but little consideration is given as to how to bring ideas together or to select one over another. This can be bewildering for group members and it is not helpful when carried across into the practice situation, in which there is a need to decide on a coherent approach and to have a rationale for doing so. I would see this difficulty in its more extreme form as the result of anxiety about competition between group members, resulting in a blanket need to treat everyone's contributions equally. But if the group has confidence that all members have valuable resources to offer and that these will emerge over time, the facilitator does not need to worry about helping the group gather its thoughts together at this stage, selecting ideas which seem especially meaningful and thereby achieving a measure of closure.

A further common pitfall is the development of an assumption by the group – particularly when it comes to the More Effortful Thinking stage – that it is the job of the facilitator to come up with an answer. If this dynamic takes hold it can be unnecessarily pressurising for the facilitator (while also offering some obvious gratifications), and get in the way of providing opportunities for the group to develop its own capacity for creative and independent thinking. The key task of the facilitator is to build the resources of the group, and if they are busy trying to come up with an answer they will not be doing this. Of course sometimes, even often, the facilitator may have helpful ideas to contribute. But it is important not to go along with the idea that the facilitator should always have the solution to the problem posed or the final word.

Last, but certainly not least, there is the question of the needs of the person generating material and the extent to which the group remains mindful of these in developing an understanding of what is put before them. It is possible for groups to get involved in an absorbing discussion, only to discover at a later point that the presenting practitioner has been left feeling misunderstood or criticised, or unable to do anything with what has been talked about. It may be that they find that the discussion develops in a way that does not address their needs given the context within which they are working, or it may be that they feel that the conversation is conducted in a way that undermines their efforts or is disregarding of their experience. An example is when the group gets involved in exploring a particular aspect of the case, let us say the nature of a female client's relationship with her son, when the presenting practitioner has said that they want to understand better what is going on in the therapeutic relationship.

It is not helpful to work to too narrow a definition of the needs of the person generating material, since reflective practice works best if staff feel able to explore ideas freely and are not overly constrained by the need to be nice about each other's work. As a starting point it is important during the Generation stage for groups to ask presenters what they want from the group, bearing in mind that when someone is struggling or stuck this may be difficult to define. A hazy or apparently inarticulate request will often still convey useful information about their needs. Next, the work in a reflective practice group should, at the bottom, always be based on an empathic alignment with the practitioner who is bringing an experience to share. Members should feel free to step away from this alignment to gain perspective on the problem, but discussion should be rooted in, and should return to, a concern with their colleague's experience as a practitioner engaged and involved in a human situation. Indeed, judgement and criticism are not helpful in reflective practice. We all know that it is one thing to comment on what we should think or do at a distance from a charged interpersonal situation; quite another when you are actually in it! So towards the end of the meeting, the discussion should be brought back to the issue set out by the presenter at the start, even if this is now seen in a new light. The needs of the practitioner in providing the best possible care to the client are the ultimate focus for reflective practice, and the next stage of the Intersubjective Model, Turning Out, ensures that this is not forgotten.

Illustration: a reflective practice group for nurses finds its way towards alignment with the needs of the presenter, thereby gaining a challenging but rewarding focus for More Effortful Thinking

I was facilitating a reflective practice group for eight nurses working in a paediatric service. This group had been meeting on a monthly basis for a couple of years. We heard from a member, Sally, who had been working with a family who had disclosed serious and sustained domestic abuse to her. Sally had been threatened on the phone by the father of the person accused of the abuse for reporting information to social services. He had said that he was going to beat her up and that he would hurt her badly because what she had done would destroy his family. She had told a senior colleague, who was not in the group, that she felt scared and wondered if she was at risk. Sally had felt anxious about being attacked when she was walking on her own to the car park after work the previous week. She had said to the colleague that she felt unexpectedly frightened and did not know whether to take her feelings seriously or not. Her colleague had reacted in a jokey way and seemed to want to change the subject. Sally said she now thought her colleague's reaction had been dismissive, but she still felt a bit silly about the whole thing.

The group shared their responses to the material and their own experiences in clinical practice of being scared or feeling on edge. This was something most could relate to because they had worked over the years with clients who were violent or who threatened violence. I did notice, however, that no one talked of an experience of being directly threatened by someone who was free to act – as opposed to someone who was in hospital or prison, for example – as Sally had done.

The group then shifted fairly quickly into questions about why the family member had behaved in a threatening way. They said things like, 'I wonder if X felt threatened or scared himself', and 'X probably wanted to protect his son'. Some members spoke about identifying with the protective feelings of the family member who had threatened Sally. They talked of imagining what it would be like if their son had

Table 8.1 Advice regarding critical issues at the More Effortful Thinking stage

Critical issue	Role of the facilitator
Premature move into an intellectual or abstract mode	Draw group back to more grounded thinking about the details of the material shared and their more immediate responses and feelings; return to the abstract mode when this has happened
Group gets stuck in a reactive, emotional mode	When emotions have been explored, indicate the need to step back and think about what is happening; be prepared to be firm about this as groups can get stuck in this mode
Ideas are applied in an overly formulaic way	Encourage curiosity about detail and complexity; bring in questions and concerns from different members; attend to the pace of discussion
Lots of competing ideas are offered; discussion remains incoherent and unintegrated	Bear in mind issues of comparison and competition in the group; if anxieties about these are less, members will be more able to integrate ideas in a way that makes clinical sense
The facilitator is expected to have all the answers	It can be gratifying as well as pressurising to be put in this position; contribute to the discussion, especially earlier on in the life of a group, but focus on encouraging members to generate their own thoughts and ideas rather than providing them yourself
The needs of the person who generated material are lost sight of	Ask the person generating material what they want/need from the group during Generation stage; base thinking in subsequent stages on empathic alignment with them; bring understanding back to question or concern raised by presenter, even if it has been reframed by the group

been accused of being violent towards a partner, and how hard it would be to see the matter clearly. Others spoke of the need to retain a sense of moral perspective; they said they hoped they would be able to keep a clear sense of the difference between right and wrong, even if this meant accepting legal action against their child. One member said, 'He probably wanted to protect his child, I would', and another, 'If my child had done what Y had done I would still report them – it's about doing the right thing'.

The group then started to think of what Sally could do to ensure her safety. My sense at this point was that the group had responded in a fairly instinctive way to the material generated by their colleague, but had not really thought about what was going on – certainly not in terms of the whole situation put before them. Sally echoed my thoughts when she said that she wanted to hear more from the group about the reaction of her colleague, rather than what had gone on in the family. She was concerned about her feelings being dismissed. Why was this? Was she just being silly? She wanted to understand the interaction a bit more and what she could do about it.

There was a pause; the group seemed a bit stuck. I suggested that colleagues might find it hard to hear about more difficult emotions in relation to their work and might dismiss them as a way of protecting themselves. Sally said that she had not thought of it like that. The group started to talk about some of the differences between the staff group as represented by Sally, and the staff group to which belonged the colleague who Sally had tried to talk to about being frightened. Comments were made such as: 'We manage a lot of safeguarding and domestic abuse disclosures,' and 'They don't understand what we have to deal with'. Mary said there was a 'them and us' culture, and the group started to think of things they could do to bridge the division between both the two groups.

John then made the observation that they had, in a way, dismissed Sally's difficult feelings by shifting their focus to the family material, when the fact that she felt threatened – and with good reason – was obviously more important. Debbie said the family was important too, and John said what he meant was that he thought what Sally wanted help with was the interaction with her colleague. These issues with colleagues are often so much more stressful than the actual clinical work. Sally was sitting outside the group, but she made a humorous facial expression to indicate that John was on the right track. Mary said perhaps they had found it hard to think about Sally's fear because it was better to just pretend they were all invulnerable and nothing bad could ever happen to them. There was laughter in the group – a feeling of having really got hold of how hard it can be to hear about real difficulty and vulnerability from a colleague and why this might be. It felt like it had taken some work on Sally's and my part to achieve focus for the More Effortful Thinking stage, but we had got there in the end.

Towards the end of the group, it was possible to consider how Sally might approach a conversation with her team about taking her need to feel safe at work seriously and how to protect her over the coming weeks. She thought that if her team knew about the threat and took it seriously, she would feel better supported. Various members of the group then put forward some good ideas about how to ensure Sally's safety, and it felt as if we were on more solid ground than before in considering practical solutions.

Techniques

My usual way of facilitating the transition to the More Effortful Thinking Stage is to indicate that it is time to step back and gather thoughts together. I ask a question like: 'What do we think is happening?' Or if I feel the need to bring about a more emphatic shift: 'If we step back and take a view about what is going on, drawing on our knowledge and other ideas we might have, what do we think is happening?' This usually brings about a change of pace, and discussion automatically becomes slower and more deliberate.

The main technical question for this stage is whether to use a structured approach to thinking about the material presented, or to encourage wider exploration of concepts from across models within any given healthcare discipline, including ideas from outside the healthcare field. There are pros and cons to the two approaches. If you are working with a staff group who are finding it difficult to formulate and make sense of material, it can be helpful to use a structured model to do this and to move to a more fluid approach when the group has gained confidence. If you are working with practitioners who take more easily to this 'thinking stage', it can work well to adopt an open approach to generating ideas from early on. But it is still useful to make more systematic use of a single model from time to time in order to develop the thinking of the group. Variety is the key here: a narrow, single model approach is likely to bring a depth of understanding but not a variety of perspective; a freer, cross-disciplinary orientation is likely to bring freshness and innovation but may become somewhat unfocused.

Some reflective practice groups make use of creative methods, such as drawing, to gather together thinking at this stage. They also use these techniques to open up thinking, and I have described them more fully in the chapter on Generation. I have several colleagues who regularly take large pieces of paper and crayons or pens into groups they facilitate. I think shifting genre – from words to visual images, or from words to music or drama; or from theoretical, abstract language to something more expressive such as poetry or story – creates powerful new possibilities for meaning-making. It can also be an effective way of freeing up a group who are finding it difficult to think in any way other than the one they are used to. If you want to try a creative method pick one which appeals to you and the group; the aim here is to select a means of opening up thought and expression, and the actual technique you select does not matter too much.

You also do not have to use a full-blown method. I do not tend to incorporate creative methods into my facilitation of reflective practice, but I do quite often ask members for a visual image to convey what they are trying to get at, or to describe a situation as if those involved were characters in a story or film. It is surprising how even a small foray into the world of fantasy and make-believe can help members put something difficult but important into words. Do not be put off by some initial, but hopefully short-lived, embarrassment or inhibition; it can feel strange to start to draw in front of professional colleagues, but this diminishes when the value of opening up thinking in this way becomes apparent.

Key influences

I have been helped in understanding the mental work involved in gaining the More Effortful Thinking stage and the reluctance groups often show in moving into it by contemporary accounts of Oedipal development, and by Daniel Kahneman's (2011) book *Thinking, Fast and Slow*.

Melanie Klein and the British Object Relations School in psychoanalysis have linked the child's earliest experiences of familial relationships – and crucially the shift from two- to three-person functioning – to the growth of curiosity and, in a broader sense, to intellectual and creative maturation (Klein, 1923; Britton, 1985; Britton, 1989). Oedipal theory describes the child's gradual realisation that their mother or main carer does not belong to them exclusively, but has important relationships with others, and in particular, their father or another partner. The process of growing up requires the child to relinquish their exclusive relationship with their mother or main carer to relate to her as someone in a couple relationship – or, in the case of a single parent, as someone who has strong interests and attachments apart from their relationship with their child.

The acceptance of the parental relationship is regarded as a crucial development, which involves learning to tolerate difficult emotions but yields significant rewards. It requires the capacity to deal with feelings of exclusion and smallness, of deprivation, envy and jealousy. However, if some real mastery over these feelings is gained, the individual is considerably more able as they go on in life to learn from others because they can recognise the knowledge and skills which others possess and they do not. When it comes to triangular relationships and group situations they are more able to draw on the resources generated by the relationships of others, benefitting from the perspectives produced by these connections between other people, rather than experiencing these other relationships as a threat.

Oedipal theory has rightly been criticised for its assumption that a particular Western model of the nuclear family can be universally applied to the understanding of child development across different cultures and periods of history (Mitchell, 1974). There are now a number of accounts of Oedipal theory which have moved away from cultural stereotypes of the family and the parental relationship, and which have introduced the concept of thirdness into thinking about development, rather than the concrete and culturally specific triangle of mother, father and child (Coelho, 2016). Within these descriptions the move from a primary, two-person relationship to the acceptance of a third person or object is the key shift, whether the triangular relationship is between the child and, respectively: the parent (of either sex) and another adult, or the parent and a sibling, or a primary carer and another person, or even a parent and a new interest or activity, such as going back to work.

This theoretical tradition has given me a strong sense of the importance in reflective practice of first getting close to material – as in an engaged, up-close, two-person relationship – and then of being able to draw back and adopt a separate position in order to think, take stock, and make meaning – the equivalent of taking up the position of the third person in a triangular relationship. Jessica Benjamin calls the latter 'the third position', and she sees its vantage point as very valuable to clinical work, and particularly to developing an understanding of what is going on in the here-and-now therapeutic relationship (Benjamin, 2017). When a reflective practice group is functioning well, it is able to move, metaphorically speaking, from a two-person to a three-person mode: from immersion in practice, with all the feelings and confusion generated by lived experience of interactions at work, to something clearer and more defined, which makes use of the perspectives of group members to transform understanding of the problem.

Oedipal theory offers the possibility that More Effortful Thinking, which is based on the move from close engagement to the integration of a new perspective, can be experienced as difficult because, at a primitive level, it involves feelings of resentment and intrusion into a comfortable or known relationship, and it also requires relinquishment. Instead of a cherished relationship, the reflective practitioner may need to give up a cherished notion or view of themselves. I have found these ideas helpful in making sense of the way in which the facilitator attempting to shift the group from the reactive engagement of the Free Response stage to More Effortful Thinking can feel like a resented intruder. The move to this thinking stage is necessary for the work of the group, but it can also feel to group members like giving something up. This is usually temporary because the gains of the More Effortful Thinking stage soon emerge, but it can be intense and quite uncomfortable while it lasts.

The effort involved in this stage is also explained by Kahneman's description in *Thinking, Fast and Slow* of two distinct thinking systems involving different parts of the brain, one of which is automatic, fast and draws on previous knowledge to deal with familiar situations; the other of which is slow, considered and is brought into play when faced with novelty and complexity. In Kahneman's account, which is based on recent findings from cognitive psychology and neuroscience, Thinking Fast often happens outside of conscious awareness and is relatively effortless, and Thinking Slow requires a great deal of mental and physical work by comparison. In Kahneman's description, the two modes of thinking are quite distinct, although much of the time they work together in a low-key way; but the shift from the reactive, fast mode to more sustained and considered, analytical thinking is something which we would usually rather not undertake because of the effort involved.

I do not think that reflective practice groups regularly require such a stark change of gear, but Kahneman's account does help us understand more about the function of different thinking modes, and the experience of moving between them. It also puts pay to the idea that Thinking Fast involves harder work than slowing down to deliberate, and to the notion of reflection as an indulgent, navel-gazing activity. The sort of thinking which develops new ideas and resolves knotty problems and dilemmas has been proven to be hard, tiring work: it may be slow but it is neither relaxing nor easy.

Summary

- The More Effortful Thinking stage is about stepping back from practice material and the group's more immediate responses in order to bring together a coherent understanding, however partial, of what is going on.
- The emphasis should be on working from the ground up and using ideas where they make sense of experience, rather than the top-down and full application of a particular approach – although it may be helpful for groups to try the latter from time to time.
- Formulation is certainly part of what takes place at this stage in reflective practice, but the focus is usually on theory-practice links rather than the systematic use of a particular model; theories or concepts from any of the healthcare disciplines may be drawn upon as well as from outside usual professional discourses.
- Thinking 'outside the box' should be encouraged, such as the introduction of an idea from a book or film or from an area of interest outside of work.
- Facilitators should welcome a period of sustained, deliberate thinking by the group but not expect it to last for the majority of the meeting; research has shown that this type of cognitive activity requires a change of gear and is hard, even at times painful, work, and it is important to be realistic about how much of it a group can manage on any one occasion.
- Facilitators sometimes need to help groups get a balance between the Free Response and More Effortful Thinking stages: groups often move into an abstract mode too quickly before they have had the chance to fully explore the situation presented to them; on the other hand, they can find it difficult to step back from emotional reactions to the work and shift into a thinking mode.
- Facilitators also sometimes need to help groups get a balance between ordering material too much or too little: groups may attempt to gain mastery over material, generating overly formulaic responses at the expense of the integration of lived experience with higher-order thinking; on the other hand, it is sometimes hard to move discussion beyond a mass of competing ideas.
- Groups sometimes expect the facilitator to offer a finished formulation and provide the answer to the question of how to understand what is going on; this can be flattering but the facilitator should avoid taking up the expert position too firmly and preventing the group from developing an understanding for themselves.

- Work in a reflective practice group should always be based on an empathic alignment with the practitioner generating material, and thinking should be informed by what will help them with their practice.
- Some reflective practice groups prefer an open approach to this stage, seeing which links emerge between intuitive responding and more deliberate thought; others find it useful to apply a structured approach. In the latter case try to avoid the hasty imposition of meaning onto the material and allow for some integration of ideas generated during the Free Response Stage.
- Creative methods can be helpful in gathering together thinking at this stage: use an approach which you and the group feel reasonably comfortable with and try not to be put off by some understandable but hopefully short-lived embarrassment.

References

Benjamin, J. (2017) *Beyond doer and done to: recognition theory, intersubjectivity and the third.* London: Routledge.

Britton, R. (1989) The missing link: parental sexuality in the Oedipus complex. In *The Oedipus complex today: clinical implications.* London: Karnac Books.

Britton, R. (1985) The Oedipus complex and the depressive position. *Sigmund Freud House Bulletin,* 9: 7–12.

Coelho, N.E.Junior (2016) The origins and destinies of the idea of thirdness in contemporary psychoanalysis. *International Journal of Psycho-Analysis,* 97(4): 1105–1127.

Kahneman, D. (2011) *Thinking fast, thinking slow.* London: Penguin Books.

Klein, M. (1923) Early analysis. In *Love, guilt and reparation: and other works 1921–1945 (the writings of Melanie Klein, volume* I) (1975). London: Hogarth Press and the Institute of Psychoanalysis.

Mitchell, J. (1974) *Psychoanalysis and feminism: a radical reassessment of Freudian psychoanalysis.* London: Penguin Books.

Schon, D. (1984) *The reflective practitioner: how professionals think in action.* Farnham, Surrey: Ashgate Books Ltd.

Symington, N. (1986) *The analytic experience: Lectures from the Tavistock.* London: Free Association Books.

9 Turning Out

What is Turning Out?

The Turning Out stage is when the group considers how to apply the thinking they have done in the seminar to the outside situation. As a first step, the group asks for feedback from the person who has generated material for the seminar about how useful or not the reflections of others have been. It is then helpful to think about the external work situation for this person and the aspects of this which need to be borne in mind in making use of the work of the seminar. It may be that the situation allows for the clinician to put ideas into practice with relative ease; or it may be that there are constraints which limit what can be done – or at least need to be taken into account in moving forward; or it may be that the real-world context offers possibilities in applying the thinking of the group, leading to an opportunity or a new idea. Necessity, as the saying goes, is the mother of invention.

The group may have directed attention to what might be offered to the client in an ideal scenario, but there are likely to be limits, sometimes severe, on what can be offered. The reflective practice group may have found it helpful to think about problems according to an approach which is not shared by staff working in the service, and perhaps particularly by senior staff or supervisors. The person who has generated material may be very interested in what has been discussed but feel unsure about how to go about putting it into practice. Or an aspect of the service and the resources available may inspire an idea about what could be offered to the client which builds on previous discussions.

The aim at this stage is not so much to undertake a complete job of working out how to apply the reflections of the seminar group in practice, but to give space to the consideration of some of the key issues and thereby to remind the group that putting ideas into practice is often not a straightforward matter. Sometimes, the group will need to face up to the difficulty, or even the near impossibility, of applying the thinking of the seminar in any direct way. I have taken part in discussions in reflective practice that put group members more in touch with the needs of clients, which could not be met because of a dire lack of resource. This is a difficult situation to bear. But it is more helpful for staff to face the problem together than to avoid the issue, and leave the meeting with the sense that they ought to be doing something that it is, in fact, not possible to do. It is also sometimes the case that, although service provision may fall short, the fact that the practitioner is able to empathise with the client and acknowledge their experience makes a difference in and of itself. Empathy is a powerful force for good, and is strongly associated in the literature with positive therapeutic outcomes, even if our ability to act upon it is limited (Norcross, 2011).

If the member who has generated material has sat out while others share their reactions and try to make sense of what they have heard (the Free Response and More Effortful Thinking stages), this will be the point when they rejoin the group. What I would usually do is to ask them what it has been like listening to others talk about their experience. It is important that they are able to say if they have been upset or confused by something that has been said, as well as if they have found an idea helpful. Sometimes they will want to gain clarification or explore something more fully to help them make better use of it in the external situation. The experience of hearing others engage with their work, imagining their predicament and the different people involved, is usually a powerful and supportive one. It is valuable having a few moments at least to take it in.

It is also sometimes necessary to talk about the potential for disagreement or controversy if the group has formed a view which is at odds with that of colleagues in the relevant service. The aim in reflective practice is to develop thinking in relation to a clinical case or issue, as distinct from clinical supervision from a management or governance perspective, in which the practitioner offers an account of their work for review. Reflective practice should not compete with such external supervision arrangements. Either the ideas generated can be offered to the supervisor as helpful, alternative thoughts about what might be going on; or, where it is anticipated that this will not be welcome, the group can think about how the practitioner might reconcile different points of view for the good of the client. As an example, if the group has found it useful to think about a clinical issue from a family or systems perspective but the service is firmly rooted in cognitive-behavioural therapy (CBT) for individual clients, members might focus on developing the CBT formulation in order to take account of the impact of the family environment. If it is not possible to offer family therapy, it might be helpful to develop a collaborative understanding with the client of what underlies their difficulties that incorporates a systemic perspective. Ideas about subtle but practical alterations of this kind can be discovered at this stage, particularly when one has the resources of a group of experienced practitioners to drawn upon.

Aside from tending to the question of how to apply the thinking of the group, the Turning Out stage offers the opportunity for members to reflect on the experience of each meeting. It incorporates a review element in which members look back on what has been discussed, separating a little from it as they ready themselves to return to busy working lives. There are of course additional opportunities to do this, such as in the Looking Back stage in subsequent meetings and regular reviews. These spaces to consider past discussions allow for valuable processing of group responses, particularly the emotional reactions of members, and for meaning-making over time.

Critical issues

At this stage, the most common problem is that too little time is given to the transition out of a reflective practice group because the group has got absorbed in other things, and the Turning Out stage comes at the end. If possible, at least ten minutes should be left for this in an hour-long group, fifteen minutes in a longer one. It is particularly important that the person generating material for the groups has the opportunity to share their reactions, so if the group has time for nothing else they should ensure that they give time to this.

On the other hand, this stage should not be overworked. Sometimes I have seen too much of a focus on what to do in response to a conundrum, at the expense of opening up thinking and feeling. Reflective practice has developed in its current form partly as a corrective to overly busy and action-oriented healthcare services; and although it is important to help staff go back into these environments, the emphasis on emotional responses, intuition and creative thinking should not be sacrificed. The Turning Out stage should allow some initial thinking about how to bring reflection and practice together, but it is not the group's responsibility to come up with a detailed plan for how to do this. Instead facilitators should communicate a certain confidence that participants will be able to make use of the thinking of the seminar in their own way over time.

Occasionally ideas in a reflective practice group develop to contradict what the practitioner is doing or being required to do, and this difference cannot be ignored. For example, action will need to be taken if serious malpractice by a colleague is unearthed or it is necessary to protect a child or a vulnerable adult. This may be uncomfortable for the practitioner to address with a supervisor or senior staff in their department, in which case the group can help them think about how to do this in a constructive way. Or they may feel unable to address the situation themselves and, according to the steps outlined in Table 1 in Chapter 3, the facilitator may decide to meet with the practitioner outside the group with the possibility of liaising directly themselves with the clinical service. For example, some years ago, a colleague facilitating a group realised that social services should be told about a matter concerning a vulnerable child, although the supervisor had decided this was not the case, and the supervisee, who had brought the case to the seminar, was understandably reluctant to go against the view of their supervisor. In this instance, the reflective practice group facilitator had a conversation with the clinical supervisor outside the group, and this resulted in the supervisor making contact with social services. It is always preferable for the practitioner to take up such statutory matters themselves, and this is what the facilitator should aim for in the first instance. But if the facilitator is considering the need to act themselves in this way, they should always seek a supportive conversation with a colleague to help think things through, meet separately with the practitioner concerned to explore the situation fully and away from the constraints of a group setting, and then act if and when they consider this to be the right thing to do, letting the group know what has happened and moving to restore normal, boundaried activity as soon as is possible.

Illustration: a reflective practice group on a training day that ends with the sense that something significant has taken place without being able to name what has happened

I am going to describe the Turning Out stage of a reflective practice group which I observed on a training day. The group was made up of a combination of seven or eight social workers and clinical psychologists who were part of a larger group attending a course on the facilitation of reflective practice groups. They had met two times before on the course as a smaller group to apply the ideas presented to them in the mornings, so they had got to know each other a bit and felt they were getting the hang of things.

One of the group, Helen, came forward readily with material she wanted to share. She spoke about how she felt about a young woman who had been admitted to the residential unit where she worked. I will not give too many details about the client because it is not necessary to do so, but I will say that the client and her mother had spoken to staff in the unit many times about experiences of bullying. There was something about the way they did this which resulted in staff not knowing whether to believe them or not. It seemed like there was one story about victimisation after another. Helen opened up to the group about feelings of irritation towards the client. She thought the client wanted help from her, but that nothing she or anyone could do would be enough. She also reflected that she had worked with teenagers before who found it hard to make use of care, and she had not felt the same way.

The facilitator encouraged members of the group to share responses to the material, and they did this in a free and lively way, considering what their feelings might begin to tell them about the client's experience. As members talked about the client's situation in life the feeling of empathy for her grew. It was as if her experiences were becoming real for the group, and members were getting to know her. But something happened towards the end of the meeting: the mood in the room became heavy, and the energy level went right down. Earlier, people had had lots of thoughts and feelings in response to the material, and now, for some elusive reason, they suddenly did not have any. There were ten minutes to go, and I remember wondering whether the facilitators would finish the group early because things felt so empty.

I learnt later that, at this point, the facilitator was in a dilemma. He was someone who tends to feel a pressure to 'wrap things up' if he is running a staff group, and his impulse was to offer a formulation – something concrete for colleagues to take away. However today he wanted to have a go at not doing this, thereby encouraging group ownership of the process.

The group managed to stay with their feelings, which were flat and heavy. A couple of comments were made about the mood in the room, but members were hazy as to what was going on. The facilitator asked Helen what it had been like to hear the reflections of others. She said one or two things and then came to a more definite statement. She thought that, perhaps with this client, it was not so much about doing things to help but about being with the client and understanding her perspective. She was looking forward to seeing the client later in the week – something which had not happened before. In retrospect I wonder if being released from the pressure to act made it more possible for Helen to engage emotionally with her client.

One member said she had got a lot from Helen sharing her feelings of irritation with the client. It reminded her that we are all human and that it is alright not to like everyone we work with – or not to like them all the time. At the end of the group and just afterwards, members were struck by the feeling state they were in. They had the sense that something had happened; they had been taken over by a growing identification with the client, but were not sure about anything more than that. They spoke about the fact that if they had had the opportunity of further meetings as a group, they would have wanted to return to think about how they were feeling. Individual members would do so on their own after the group.

I thought at the time that the fact that Helen was looking forward to seeing the client represented a significant development. Something solid had been achieved, although it was difficult to grasp what had happened because of the heavy, unresolved feeling in the room. But the shift was there nevertheless. This example shows how important work with feelings is for healthcare staff. It can be difficult to put this emotional work into words of explanation, or even simple description, certainly after a one-off discussion. However, over time, making sense of the learning gained within the group in this way does become possible.

Technique

The Turning Out stage is a relatively short, transitional stage and, generally, techniques are not used for it. I have heard from facilitators who invite the group to prepare a brief written record together at the end of the meeting. This enables shared ownership of the processing and review element of this stage, which then becomes a regular part of the group's process, at the same time as producing a useful summary for later review. This can be helpful, but should not replace open discussion of the sort that members would prefer to keep out of a written summary. I prefer to write a written record of this kind with the group at six-monthly review points, thinking together with members about how we might choose to let managers know what we have been working on, and keeping the end of a reflective practice group free in between times for whatever comes up.

Summary

- The Turning Out stage involves making a bridge between the thinking that has gone on inside the seminar and the real-world conditions of practice which influence its application and offer both constraints and possibilities.

- Feedback from the person who has generated material for the seminar should be sought as to how useful or not they have found discussions; if they have been sitting out during the Free Response and More Effortful Thinking stages, this is the point at which they rejoin the group.
- The group may on occasion need to face up to the fact that it is difficult to make use of the reflections of members because of limited resources, in which case it is better to acknowledge frustrations and disappointments together than to pretend that things are possible which are not, and thereby set practitioners up to fail. It is thought that supporting one another in the face of such difficulties makes it more possible to offer empathy to clients, reducing the need for defensive disconnection from clients' experiences of seeking help within overstretched healthcare services.
- The Turning Out stage tends to be given too little time because it comes at the end of the meeting; at least ten minutes in an hour-long group should be kept for it and priority is given to hearing what it has been like for the person who has generated material for the group to listen to the responses of others.
- However this transitional stage should not be overworked: after all, the emphasis in reflective practice is on opening up thinking and feeling in response to clinical work, rather than the production of a detailed action plan.
- Occasionally the facilitator may decide they need to act outside the group, usually in accordance with legal requirements (for example, statutory child protection legislation); according to the procedure set out in Table 1 of Chapter 3, the facilitator should keep the group informed about what is happening, talk things through with a colleague before taking action, meet outside the constraints of the group setting to explore the matter further with the practitioner concerned, inform a manager if they judge this to be the right thing to do and then move to restore the normal, boundaried activity of the group as soon as possible.
- The Turning Out stage exists to bring each meeting to an end and help members orient towards activities outside; the facilitator does not need to worry about completing all lines of inquiry, but should aim instead to model an ongoing process of reflection and discovery as members apply ideas from the group to their experiences in practice.

References

Norcross, J. (Ed.) (2011) *Psychotherapy relationships that work: evidence-based responsiveness* (2nd ed.). Oxford: Oxford University Press.

10 Conclusion

In 1625 Francis Bacon (1985) famously wrote 'Reading makes us a full man; Conference a ready man; and Writing an exact man'. As a result of writing this book I have grown clearer and more precise in some areas relating to reflective practice than before and less clear in others. I have also learnt a great deal, reading and conferring with colleagues, as well as writing, to explore ideas and link them with practice. This learning has come about through having to be explicit about how I facilitate reflective practice groups and account for my approach, through reading relevant theory and empirical research to check facts and consolidate background thinking – sometimes to discover that certain aspects of the model required development in unforeseen ways and through coming up against all that I do not know about a large and hard-to-define subject. In this concluding chapter, I will summarise the main differences in how I think about and facilitate reflective practice groups now compared to when I started to write this book.

Initially I was reluctant to present a model because I did not want to prescribe practice either for myself or other people. Reflective practice is, after all, intended as a freeing process, helping healthcare professionals to reconnect with their feelings and their innate wisdom and creative capacities. It seemed counter-intuitive to tell people how to do it, certainly in any detail, and I preferred to loosely offer suggestions, which could then be taken up in whatever way seemed useful. I now think I was confusing means and ends. The overall aim of reflective practice may be to open up thinking about clinical practice, but it is only likely to be helpful to offer ideas as to how to go about doing this. In an area which can be unhelpfully enigmatic and open-ended, presentation of a model to potential facilitators of reflective practice groups gives something to work from, which they are, of course, free to accept or adapt or reject.

I began to put together the Intersubjective Model by describing the key elements of what I already did. It had at its core, first, acknowledgement and exploration of emotional responses to work in healthcare and the encouragement of associative and creative links, and second, a more disciplined effort at making sense of the clinical material presented and weaving into this an understanding the explorative products of the first stage. These became the Free Response and More Effortful Thinking stages in the model. The group contracting stage, and the transitional stages from the busy, pressured world of work in healthcare to the reflective mode and back again, were also part of my existing practice and were included from the start. There were a further three steps to building the model. I developed the presentation stage according to the question of how material should be produced to be of use in a reflective practice group, and therefore renaming it the Generation stage. I made the change from consideration of organisational dynamics as a background to a foreground issue, incorporating Contracting and Review at the Organisational Level as a foundational stage of the model. And I expanded the Looking Back stage: follow-through from previous discussions had been something I did occasionally, but as I wrote about building the thinking resources of groups over time, rather than aiming to wrap up problems in one-off meetings, it came to seem like an important regular part of the process.

The model is now finished, or at least more finished, which is satisfying. But there is a risk that by filling it out something of its essence has been lost. I have tried to write in such a way as to convey the core aspects of reflective practice as I see it, in the form of an opening out process, encouraging a live engagement with the material brought, and a process of gathering together, whereby meaning is made in some form or another. It is often not possible to carry out all of the six regular activities each time a group meets, and it is preferable for a group to do fewer things well, rather than rush around all the stages each time. I hope that facilitators will feel free to relate to the model by the spirit and not the letter, using it to develop their own approach and aiming for flow through the essentials of each stage rather than slavish obedience to the scheme.

It has been heartening to read the research on clinical supervision relevant to the development of reflective practice in healthcare, even if this leaves more questions than answers. When I trained in the 1990s, there was barely any research looking at the impact of supervision on clinical practice. Supervision was viewed as an important but subsidiary activity, secondary to, and supportive of, clinical practice. Accordingly, findings related to therapy and the therapeutic relationship tended to be loosely applied to thinking about supervision and the supervisory relationship. This makes intuitive sense, of course. But as research in the area grows and we learn more about the nature and impact of supervision in healthcare, it will surely emerge as an interesting and significant topic in its own right.

We now have ample evidence of the positive effects of supervision on staff well-being and job satisfaction, and we also have available a handful of high-quality investigations, all of which have control conditions, into the impact of supervision on clinical outcomes (Bambling et al., 2006; Berg, Hansson & Hallberg, 1994: Bradshaw, Butterworth & Mairs, 2007; Kellett et al., 2014). The latter shows that supervision is associated with positive clinical effects across a range of healthcare services and settings. The supervisors who participated in these studies tended to draw on a specific model of supervision in which they had received training, although the evidence does not suggest that any one model or type of supervision is more effective than another. It is worth drawing attention to this because, generally in healthcare services, clinical supervisors do not use a model. I wonder whether, as in the view that use of a therapeutic model is effective because it aids the formation of the therapeutic alliance, drawing on a model in supervision gives the supervisor confidence in what they are doing and enables collaborative working with the client and a shared sense of purpose (Norcross, 2011). A model of supervision may, therefore, be more important as a means to an end than as an end to itself – the end, in this case, being a collaborative and purposeful supervisory relationship. If this is the case, I hope the Intersubjective Model of Reflective Practice Groups will prove helpful.

The quality of the supervisory relationship comes through as particularly important in the growing research literature (Beinart & Clohessy, 2017). It is strongly associated with supervisees' satisfaction with supervision, which is not, of course, the same thing as effectiveness in supervision. But it does look as if there is a relationship between supervisees' satisfaction and their willingness to be open about practice, which is a necessary first step to effective supervision. For example, there is an interesting study which shows that when practitioners are relatively dissatisfied with the supervisory relationship they are correspondingly less likely to be open in supervisory discussions about areas of distress and difficulty in their work (Ladany et al., 1996). Reluctance on the part of practitioners to disclose areas of uncertainty and difficulty in supervision and to report mistakes is known to be widespread. If the quality of the supervisory relationship is a key to a more open examination of practice, it will be well worthwhile learning more about what makes the difference to supervisees' decisions to disclose or not.

The emphasis on the quality of the supervisory relationship in determining the success or otherwise of supervision brings me back with renewed interest to an early influence: Gosling and Turquet's (1967) classic essay *The Training of General Practitioners*. This contains excellent advice for the facilitator of a reflective practice group about the relationship between the group leader and members of the group. Gosling and Turquet outline their approach to running Balint groups for doctors in the 1950s. Their aims are broadly described as human, with the implication that medicine can be dehumanising, and are further defined as 'the examination of the doctor-patient relationship and the transactions it contains'. The recommendation is for the facilitator to pay particular attention to the regulation of distance in the clinical encounter: the question of how close or far away the healthcare practitioner is, in mental terms, from their patient. They should be sufficiently engaged to understand and empathise with their patient, but not so close as to lose perspective and end up in the same boat – feeling as hopeless as the patient complaining of sadness and isolation does, or as overwhelmed as the patient who talks of being intolerably burdened.

The facilitator, according to Gosling and Turquet, should embody this task in their own attitude to the group, keeping a balance between empathic engagement and the maintenance of enough distance to have a sense of perspective on what is going on in the group. The facilitator will need proper support in the work because they will be subject to the emotional pushes and pulls of colleagues who are working in pressured and sometimes highly charged human situations. They should, for example, be able to tolerate regressed behavior on the part of the group; this, Gosling and Turquet remind us, can be a healthy temporary response in a reasonably safe and trusting group to the experience of distress and difficulty. It can also be unhealthy, if it has a destructive edge to it and lasts over-long, in which case the facilitator will need support to recognise what is going on and act accordingly. In my view, this support should consist of supervision for the work of facilitating reflective practice groups, perhaps in the form of a network of peers and wider organisational support, by which I mean the sense that the work aligns with service aims and objectives, and is actively valued by managers and colleagues.

Supervision helps the facilitator think about the position they are taking up in the group, and the extent to which this is either overly detached or overly involved. Wider organisational support prevents the facilitator from isolation in the work, which can result in an unhelpful need for popularity and approval from group members. In a study of the needs of staff working in a secure unit for people with a diagnosis of personality disorder, I suggested a link between the sense of isolation experienced by staff, and indeed stigmatisation by association with the patient group, and their enmeshment as a staff team (Kurtz & Turner, 2007). It felt as if it was them against the world, and they must stick together whatever. Staff talked in interviews about how this meant they chose not to pick each other up on issues, such as getting too close to patients, even when they needed to do so.

Organisational support is certainly starting to emerge as an additional key factor in the success or otherwise of supervision and reflective practice. Overall one of a tiny number of randomised control studies into the effectiveness of clinical supervision, and in this case of reflective supervision in a group format, yielded disappointing results (White & Winstanley, 2010). This was a large and well-designed study, evaluating a reflective group intervention for nurses preceded by intensive training for supervisors. It was conducted across 17 adult mental health services in nine different locations and incorporated measures of both clinical outcome and patient satisfaction for 170 patients. The control arm of the study consisted of services in which supervision was not routinely available. But in interviews and diary accounts, practitioners receiving supervision said that the attitude of middle managers towards the intervention was often mistrustful and even hostile, particularly when there was the possibility of uncovering instances of mismanagement. The authors concluded that this got in the way of staff attending and benefitting from supervision. This middle management group, as opposed to practitioners and senior managers, were the least likely to receive supervision themselves.

The experiences of facilitators of setting up reflective practice groups also suggest that organisational support is crucial in determining whether a group gets off the ground or not, and that ambivalence at the service level towards reflective practice is widespread and obstructive. I am now of the view that, although reflective practice can be a real force for good in clinical services, it may be unhelpful to proceed when the level of ambivalence at the service level, often unacknowledged, towards staff opening up and connecting with the human experience is too high. Reflective practice serves to put healthcare staff in touch with their feelings towards the clients they work with, and towards their colleagues, to whom they naturally look to for support and guidance. If the ethos of the service is not aligned with this relational goal, if for example, it aims for the volume of through-put rather than empathic connection and therapeutic effectiveness, reflective practice is likely to be viewed as interference. Pressing ahead with it in such conditions can make the situation worse and not better for practitioners, setting them at odds with the overall aims of the service.

Facilitators should assess the level of organisational support for reflective practice before they embark on a group, both for the sake of the practitioners involved and their own. It is a lonely burden carrying the torch for reflective practice and the values it represents in an unreflective, or an anti-reflective, service. One also risks becoming part of the problem, attempting to mop up practitioners' distress and disturbance, rather than getting senior staff within the organisation to address difficulties. Future research would do well to investigate the impact of reflective practice through an intervention which included organisational support as a key element.

This support would, of course, consist of practical aspects, such as the regular provision of a private room and the arrangement of rotas to enable consistent attendance of nursing staff. But I would also like to see this support given in the form of participation in reflective practice at different levels of the organisation, that is, in the form of an intervention in which reflective practice groups for managers ran alongside groups for ground-level staff. The pressures on managers in healthcare are acute, and they carry a great deal of responsibility under high levels of scrutiny. This is perhaps particularly the case for middle managers, who have considerable responsibilities but less power than more senior staff. This was the group that White and Winstanley (2010) found to be least likely to receive supervision and support themselves, and whose attitude towards the open examination of practice in supervision was unhelpfully mistrustful.

It is easy to see how managers of healthcare services can become anxious and risk-averse, afraid themselves of admitting to mistakes, doubts and uncertainties or of having these exposed by ground-level staff, and can resort to defensive strategies, such as distancing themselves from the human problems of the service. How are defensive, cut-off managers to support staff in opening up about dilemmas and mistakes? How can they sympathise with the emotions and interpersonal pressures produced by the work, if they are busy pretending that they are not feeling anything themselves? It would be useful to evaluate an intervention aiming to embed reflective practice at all levels of the organisation. I believe that the well-being of healthcare leaders is a neglected area, and that high levels of pressure and scrutiny affect their openness to thinking in an un-defensive and compassionate way about the needs of patients and staff, which is crucial to the development of good clinical practice. But further work is needed to establish evidence for this.

Last but by no means least, the importance of psychological safety in developing reflective practice, both at the group and organisational level, has been brought home to me through research carried out alongside writing this book. The calibration of the atmosphere of trust and safety in a reflective practice group is a continuous, live process for members – even if not conscious or explicitly referred to. I have also come to accept a certain amount of anxiety as an integral part of the process of reflecting on practice in healthcare, whereas, beforehand, I thought that if a group was going well, members would not feel anxious. This now seems unrealistic. After all, the human work we do involves us as people and not just as practitioners. The way we relate to clients and colleagues when we are up against human suffering says a lot about us as individuals, whether we like it or not. It is inevitable that talking about our practice in any real detail, letting others know what happened, rather than what we wish had happened, will feel exposing. This is especially the case in healthcare systems which are increasingly impersonal and bureaucratic, and where open talking about lived experiences of practice is less familiar than it should be.

I have supervised two exploratory studies of experiences of reflective practice groups for trainee clinical psychologists which looked at influences on clinical practice and ways in which participants changed how they thought about clients (Biggins, 2019; Loveder, 2017). Interviewees in both studies described a high level of awareness of the atmosphere of trust and safety in the group, monitoring responses to the disclosures of others to decide whether to open up about areas of practice about which they were troubled or unsure. Assessment of the level of safety in the group was ongoing, a dynamic process whereby trust was built as members got to know one another, but was continuously renegotiated in small ways and was not ever established once and for all. In a productive group, interviewees also alluded to a continuing sense of risk. Learning about clinical practice involved moving out of a comfort zone to explore an area of vulnerability or uncertainty. It should feel, at least a little bit, risky. From this I take the idea that a reflective practice group should be safe enough to facilitate exploration on the part of members, but not so safe that curiosity and adventurousness are stifled and constrained.

The concept of psychological safety has emerged within the field of management and business studies over the past twenty years, largely as a way of developing effective feedback mechanisms within high-risk industries, such as car and aviation, and thereby reducing errors (Edmondson & Verdin, 2018). The safer staff are to air problems and report mistakes, and to discuss these with senior colleagues and not just amongst peers, the more able the organisation is to act on information to improve systems and procedures. An accepting, non-blaming working environment is thought to be a significant factor in developing an organisational culture in which staff can think together in a non-defensive way about the work they do. The creation of a reflexive work culture of this sort obviously requires confident leadership and, in particular, the ability to distinguish between acceptable levels of error and more serious mistakes which require a stronger response. An anxious manager will conflate the two and react to any little thing which goes awry; an overly relaxed manager will not be sufficiently aware when something is wrong and they ought to intervene.

There is an important difference between the types of mistakes humans make in healthcare services and the industries which have given rise to the concept of psychological safety. On the car production line or in the cockpit of an airplane, it may be helpful to take a non-blaming approach and accept the fact of human error to improve feedback mechanisms. But the simple fact is that the fewer mistakes that are made, the better. In healthcare, and particularly in psychological and mental health services, practitioners are working on and through relationships, and this produces different kinds of successes and failures. If they are emotionally engaged in their work, they react to individual clients and the atmosphere of their environment. They will be asked by clients to tend to areas of interpersonal difficulty, and these difficulties will not remain abstract but will be directly experienced in the relationship with the practitioner. They will not just hear about the problem; they will, to an extent, live it. This can feel messy and as if things are going wrong. But sometimes in human services, things need to go wrong to go right. The reflective practitioner will then draw back from what is happening and proceed on the basis of a deeper understanding of the client's needs. Success in this context is a relationship which has been tried and tested, in which difficulties have been explored and to some extent lived out, but in the end, practitioner and client have found their way to something better.

This is known in the psychoanalytic literature as re-enactment, and there is a recognition that small-scale re-enactments are part and parcel of engaged therapeutic work and, if recognised and understood, become grist to the therapeutic mill (Casement, 2002). What matters is that the clinician is aware of what is going on, and able to think about it with the client's best interests in mind. Indeed it is likely to be more of a problem if a practitioner is so afraid of making a mistake that they remain disconnected from their clients, than if they get something wrong and manage to learn from the experience. I would also argue that large-scale enactments on the part of individual staff or staff groups, which are a matter for serious concern, can be prevented by an open and thoughtful attitude towards small-scale re-enactments. This would be another fruitful area for future research, and would help provide a case for the value of reflexivity at all levels of the healthcare organisation.

To promote psychological safety in healthcare, managers need to be able to tell the difference between practitioners who make mistakes in the context of engaged and ultimately effective clinical practice and more fundamental problems – either in the individual practitioner or in the service culture and context. The boundary between these two types of difficulty can be a grey one, and managers need to be able to contain their anxiety in order to establish which it is. But the well-supported and reflective healthcare manager will be open-minded and thoughtful about this distinction. An alternative is a top-down approach, which results in staff simply covering up their real experiences of clinical practice. This is driven, ultimately, by anxiety about avoiding an error. I believe we should take seriously the pressures on managers which get in the way of developing reflective and creative ways of running healthcare services, and offer them, along with clinical practitioners, the support and thinking space to resist them.

References

Bacon, F. (1985) *The essays.* London: Penguin Classics.

Bambling, M., King, R., Raue, P., Schweitzer, R. & Lambert, W. (2006) Clinical supervision: its influence on client-rated working alliance and client symptom reduction in the brief treatment of major depression. *Psychotherapy Research*, 16(3): 317–331.

Beinart, H. & Clohessy, S. (2017) *Effective supervisory relationships: best evidence and practice.* Chichester, West Sussex: John Wiley & Sons Ltd.

Berg, A., Hansson, U.W. & Hallberg, I.R. (1994) Nurses' creativity, tedium and burnout during 1 year of clinical supervision and implementation of individually planned nursing care: comparison between a ward for severely demented patients and a similar control ward. *Journal of Advanced Nursing*, 20(4): 742–749.

Biggins, A. (2019) *Does group reflective practice change practitioners' understanding of clients? An Interpretative Phenomenological Analysis of the impact of monthly reflective practice groups within clinical psychology training.* Unpublished Dissertation; University of Leicester.

Bradshaw, T., Butterworth, A. & Mairs, H. (2007) Does structured clinical supervision during psychosocial intervention education enhance outcome for mental health nurses and the service users they work with? *Journal of Psychiatric and Mental Health Nursing*, 14(1): 4–12.

Casement, P. (2002) *Learning from our mistakes: beyond dogma in psychoanalysis and psychotherapy.* London: Routledge.

Edmondson, A.C. & Verdin, P.J. (2018) The strategic imperative of psychological safety and organizational error management. In Hagen, J.U. (Ed.) *How could this happen? Managing errors in organizations.* Cham, Switzerland: Palgrave MacMillan.

Gosling, R. & Turquet, P.M. (1967) The training of general practitioners. In Gosling, R., Miller, D.H., Woodhouse, D. & Turquet, P.M. *The use of small groups in training.* Hertfordshire: Codicote Press.

Kellett, S., Wilbram, M., Davis, C. & Hardy, G. (2014) Team consultancy using cognitive analytic therapy: a controlled study in assertive outreach. *Journal of Psychiatric and Mental Health Nursing,* 21(8): 687–697.

Kurtz, A. & Turner, T. (2007) An exploratory study of the needs of staff who care for offenders with a diagnosis of personality disorder. *Psychology and Psychotherapy: Theory, Research and Practice,* 80: 421–435.

Ladany, N., Hill, C.E., Corbett, M.M. & Nutt, E.A. (1996) Nature, extent and importance of what psychotherapy trainees do not disclose to their supervisors. *Journal of Counselling Psychology,* 43(1): 10–24.

Loveder, M. (2017) *Does reflective practice impact upon clinical outcomes and if so, how? A grounded theory study of how trainee clinical psychologists experience the effect of a reflective practice group on their clinical work.* Unpublished Dissertation; University of Leicester.

Norcross, J. (Ed.) (2011) *Psychotherapy relationships that work: evidence-based responsiveness* (2nd ed.). Oxford: Oxford University Press.

White, E. & Winstanley, J. (2010) A randomised controlled trial of clinical supervision: selected findings from a novel Australian attempt to establish the evidence base for causal relationships with quality of care and patient outcomes, as an informed contribution to mental health nursing practice development. *Journal of Research in Nursing,* 15(2): 151–167.

Index

Page numbers in italics refer to figures. Page numbers in bold refer to tables.

activity 52, 54; organisational consultation 35; organisational context 44; phenomenal aspect 34–5; privacy and confidentiality 36–7, 44, 47, 51; purpose 35–6; purpose of contracting 51; record keeping 43–4, 54; regression 47–8; reviews 48, 53; safety and trust 37–9, 44, 52, 53; space and time 39–40; techniques 50; types of group 35; value of contracting 52

Contracting and Review at the Organisational Level 17–32; activities **22**; advice 19; aim 17–18, **22**, 31–2; anxieties of staff 20, 29; bewilderment and frustration 17; communications and feedback 18, 19, 31; coordination 18–19; critical issues 21–5, **22**; decision making 25, **27**; defensive preoccupation with external issues 24, 30; knowledge and understanding 19; liaison across groups 23, 27; organisational obstructions 19–20; organisational theory 17; organisation threat 23–4; practitioners 19; productive anxieties 20; psychology services 25; Rice social systems theory 22; social defence system 20–1, 28–30, 32; staff working experience 21; stakeholders and senior staff attitudes 21–2, 30–1; supervisory relationship quality 31; support and infrastructure 24, 28, 32; training 25–6; transference reactions 21; trust *vs.* efficiency 23; value 28

countertransference responses 110, **113**
critical thought 3
The Culture of Speed (Tomlinson) 69, 75

decision making, in reflective practice groups 36, **46**, 53, 81, 142
defensive practice 7, 20, 29, 77
defensive preoccupation 24, 30
Dewey, J. 3
digital technologies 1, 69, 75
disillusionment 6–7
distrust 6, 30

Do No Harm (Marsh) 98
DSM-V 100

educational philosophy 9
Edwards, D. 30, 31
Effective Supervisory Relationships (Beinart and Clohessy) 79
emotional literacy 5
emotional responses 82, 97, 99, 101–3, 105, 121, 141
errors 2, 146; human 147, 148; of judgement 98
existential aspect, of work groups 34

facilitators 143–5; anxieties of 48–50, 148; in group 37–8, 43, 53; Looking Back stage 71–2; More Effortful Thinking stage 122–3, 131; at organisational level 22–3, 28, 31, 32; Turning In stage 55–6, 58, 62
'facticity' 91–2
Free Response stage 96–114; advice **107**; aim 96; anxiety about personal exposure 105–6; automatic reactions 97–8; close down thinking 103–4; countertransference responses 110; creative methods 111–12, 114; critical issues from practice 103–7; curiosity and spontaneity 96; diagnostic systems 100; emotional responses 97, 99, 101–3, 105; errors of judgement 98; facilitator 106, 113–14; freer response in human services 97, 100, 105, 112, 113; grounded theory 106; illustration 101–3; immediate responses and associations 96, 99, 106; key influences 109–12, **113**; learning 99–100; legitimacy and authority 109; obstructions 101; opportunity to reconnect 97; overhasty adoption of action plan 101; overreliance on abstract 101, 113; practitioners experience 104; psychodynamic observational method 111; psychological formulation 100–1; rationale 97, **98**; risk in explorative mode 104; sitting out technique 96–7, 107–8; technical language

Printed in Great Britain
by Amazon